# The Literature of Gossip

## *Nine English Letterwriters*

BY ELIZABETH DREW

DISCOVERING POETRY

POETRY:
*A Modern Guide*

THE NOVEL:
*A Modern Guide to Fifteen English Masterpieces*

THE LITERATURE OF GOSSIP:
*Nine English Letterwriters*

# The Literature of Gossip

*Nine English Letterwriters*

ELIZABETH DREW

NEW  YORK

W · W · NORTON & COMPANY · INC ·

FIRST EDITION

Library of Congress Catalog Card No. 64-17512


Published simultaneously in the Dominion of
Canada by George J. McLeod Limited, Toronto

Printed in the United States of America
for the Publishers by the Vail-Ballou Press, Inc.

1 2 3 4 5 6 7 8 9

*To Wylie and Lucy Sypher*
*with much affection and gratitude*

# Contents

# Illustrations

# Acknowledgments

For the reproduction of portraits, I gratefully acknowledge permission from: The National Portrait Gallery, London, for Swift, Cowper, and Lamb; Admiral of the Fleet the Earl Mountbatten of Burma for Dorothy Osborne; Lord Bute for Lady Mary Wortley Montagu; Wilmarth Sheldon Lewis, Farmington, Connecticut, for Horace Walpole; The National Trust, administrator of Carlyle's House, Chelsea, for Jane Carlyle.

In addition I have to thank the following for permission to use quotations from letters as they appear in: Robert Halsband, *Lady Mary Wortley Montagu,* Oxford University Press, 1956; Alfred McKinley Terhune, *Edward FitzGerald,* Yale University Press, 1946; and the Harvard University Press, publishers of *The Letters and Private Papers of W. M. Thackeray,* edited by Gordon Ray (volume III, 1946).

# The Literature of Gossip

THE STUDY of literature is the examination of the many and fascinating ways in which life gets itself transmuted into that other order of being: art. Whether it be drama, poetry, fiction, biography, autobiography, essay, the raw substance of living experience becomes shaped into some formal structure. However unconscious of it the reader may be, nevertheless the writer has selected and arranged and lighted his materials in a conscious way; he has deliberately fashioned it for its effect on a public audience.

But one form of writing is exempt from this deliberate patterning process: the familiar letter. Of course many writings in letter form have been intended for publication, but they are not our province here. It is true that among the letter-writers in this volume, Horace Walpole was always very well aware of the value his correspondence would have in the future. As he said himself: "Nothing gives so just an idea of an age as genuine letters; nay history waits for its last seal from them." But fortunately while he certainly always had one ear cocked towards posterity, the other was never forgetful of the person whom he was talking to on paper. That is what distinguishes the true gossip. Familiar letters are written originally for an audience of one. They are regardless of fame and futurity. It takes two to write a letter as much as it takes two to make a quarrel. A letter lives only because someone wrote it for someone else to read it. As Byron said: "It is the only device for combining solitude and good company." It is a person-to-person communication. Direct "self-expression," so dangerous in conscious art, is of the very essence of a good letter; personality is its hallmark. Individuals who have achieved the greatest fame in this truly "unpremeditated art" have always been highly intelligent, interested in and curious about the world around them and the variety of people they meet or hear of in it. They read much; they observe and listen and comment with wit and wisdom. Obviously the word "gossip" in my title does not mean that the material of good letters can ever be mere insignificance and chatter. "Gossip" has an older meaning too, with its suggestion of the close intimacy and friendliness which links the regular exchangers of letters. But it is true that the inspired scribbler always has the gift for gossip in our common usage too; he or she can always inspire the commonplace with an uncommon flavor, and transform trivialities by some original grace or sympathy or humor or affection.

This essential of imparting an immediate intimate vivid presence by the power of the written word is a literary gift independent of anything else. Some people famous for their creative literary genius, like Keats or Byron or Dickens, write wonderful letters; while others, like Wordsworth or Shelley or George Eliot, strike not a single spark, and communicate nothing in the way of responsive warmth and sociability. And it is a gift shared equally by men and women. Indeed it is the only form of writing in which women have equaled men in achievement. This is natural, since the majority of women have always centered their lives in close personal relationships; their engrossing problems are those of their immediate human environment. Hence, if a woman have the necessary gifts, the letter is her perfect medium. Some of the best men letter-writers, indeed have been rather unmasculine men, like Horace Walpole and Cowper and FitzGerald; men who had no independent professions to absorb their energies. Men, however, have always combined the gift of gossip with some distinction, or at least busy occupation, with other forms of writing, whereas the brilliant women letter-writers live today simply because their personalities still glow through their correspondence, though their subject matter may often be of the most frail and ephemeral substance.

How frail and ephemeral too is the material substance of letters, which makes their very survival so hazardous. Print has a permanence of its own, though it may not be much worth preserving, but a letter! Conveyed by uncertain transportation, over which the sender has no control; committed to a single individual who may be careless or inappreciative; left to the mercy of future generations, of families maybe anxious to suppress the past, of the accidents of removals and house-cleanings, or of mere ignorance. How often it has been by the veriest chance that they survive at all. When the seventeenth-century statesman and essayist, Sir William Temple, died in 1699, his private papers, including the letters his wife had written to him before their marriage, when she was Dorothy Osborne, went to a relative living in a Suffolk village. They were inherited by her son, a country clergyman, and from him went to his brother, vicar of a nearby parish. Having no heirs, he left his property to his deceased wife's sister, who was married to his curate. It was her son who brought them, in 1836, to the notice of a biographer of Temple, but the letters were not published in full until 1888, when they had passed through the hands of six owners, and two hundred and thirty years had elapsed since the last of them had been sent by Dorothy to her lover. Or take the story of Lady Mary Wortley Montagu's love letters to Francesco Algarotti, written between 1736 and 1741. By 1817 six of them were in the possession of a Dr. Aglietti of Brescia, who had edited Algarotti's writings and owned his manuscript letters. Since many of these were to English correspondents, Aglietti thought of finding a market for them in London. At the suggestion of Byron, to whom he showed them, they were all finally bought by John Murray, Byron's publisher. Byron, who was a great admirer of Lady Mary, called Murray's attention to the letters from her: "They are very pretty and passionate . . . Algarotti seems to have treated her ill; but she was much his senior, and all women are used ill—or say so, whether they are or not." Murray did not use the collecton, but twenty years later, hearing that Lady Mary's great-grandson was editing a complete edition of her writings, he remembered Byron's recommendation and generously sent them to Lord Wharncliffe for inclusion. They were returned at once, the family having no wish that their distinguished but rather disturbing ancestress should appear in so human but undignified a situation. The letters remained buried in the Murray archives. Twenty-four more turned up in Venice in 1850, and finally found their way to the Bodleian in 1938. But neither the letters nor the crucial episode in Lady Mary's life that they memorialize were noticed until the biography by Professor Robert Halsband appeared in 1956.

It is not surprising that so many thousands of letters from Horace Walpole should survive, as he was careful to impress upon his correspondents to keep them, yet even so, hundreds were lying forgotten in libraries and in country houses until Mr. Wilmarth Lewis, with his genius for pursuit, nosed them out. And how strange it is that Coleridge, most disorderly and careless of men, in his many moves and upheavals should have kept all of Lamb's letters to him from their early youth onwards. But on the other side what gaps remain! We have none of Temple's letters to Dorothy Osborne, or those of Stella to Swift, and we know from Swift's notebooks that on an earlier visit to England between 1707 and 1709, he wrote fifteen journal letters to "the ladies" in Ireland and had eleven in return, and these have all vanished. Or there are all those letters of Jane Austen to her sister, which must have been the most intimate and personal of all her writings, and which Cassandra destroyed after Jane's death.

The natural instinct of survivors to preserve the privacies of the dead is no doubt an admirable one, and the ethical arguments for suppression will always be debated. Yet surely it is really only a question of the passing of time. The scandals or indiscretions or confessions that are a hundred years old lose all power to hurt the writer or others. Indeed one great charm of letters for the reader in the present is to meet the personalities of the past in their full humanity. To know their secrets or imperfections only makes them more human and more like ourselves, so that we give them more of our sympathy and understanding. And we judge such disclosures in perspective, in their due proportion to the total experience the letters reveal. For while personality is the root from which all the life of good letters springs, that personality is necessarily involved with the life of his time. It may be with its public events, and then we get a new perspective on history, as it comes to us intertwined with ordinary daily doings and colored by the character of its reporter. On October 30, 1712 Swift writes to Stella: "Duke Hamilton gave me a pound of snuff today, admirable good. . . . It cost me a quarter of an hour of his politick, which I was forced to hear." The next letter opens:

> Before this comes to your hands, you will have heard of the most terrible accident that hath almost ever happened. This morning at 8, my man brought me word that Duke Hamilton had fought with Lord Mohun, and killed him . . . while the Duke was over him Mohun shortening his sword stabb'd him in at the shoulder to the heart . . .

Then follows an account of Swift's tender personal concern for the Duchess, "she has moved my very soul," and he has been with her for two hours. Or in contrast to such tragic happenings, we watch the development of the South Sea Bubble as it tempted the indiscreet and financially ignorant Lady Mary, or hear Horace Walpole describe how the first time a company of aristocratic amateurs performed a play at Drury Lane, the rage to see it was so great that the House of Commons adjourned at 3 o'clock in the afternoon so that members might attend.

This perhaps concerns manners rather than history, and the letters of the men and women in this book create the English background in great variety for over two hundred years: the glitter of courts and high society in Lady Mary and Horace Walpole and Byron, the village settings of Cowper and Fitz-Gerald, the bourgeois London of Swift and of the Carlyles, the bohemian city life of Lamb and his friends. Occasionally we watch dramas full of suspense: When will Dorothy Osborne's romance have a happy ending? What will happen when Vanessa follows Swift to Ireland? How soon will Mrs. Unwin find Lady Austen's pursuit of Cowper unbearable? Can the Byron marriage possibly work out? But these are only the highlights of what holds our interest throughout. For just as personal relationships are the basis for the literature of gossip, so they are the basis for most of the lives of every later reader; and the delight we take in familiar and familial letters is in finding in so many different ages and in so many classes and callings, the problems and situations known to most of us in our own experience.

We share the lives of these men and women we come to know so well. We see them in their public lives, or in family groups, in routine duties and occupations or in close intimacies; in their triumphs and their failures and their mistakes, their squabbles and reconciliations, their happiness or grief or despair. But the dominant emotion generated throughout is the steady atmosphere of personal affection which hovered around them as they wrote and is woven into the texture of their writing. They may be telling of their hatreds and irritations, they may describe their enemies or their social disasters, their mood may be vitriolic or disillusioned, but nevertheless they are writing to someone to whom they can unload their hearts, or to whom they themselves wish to bring comfort or gaiety or the warmth of remembrance. We feel closer to letter-writers than to any other craftsmen in language, and that is because they practice what Virginia Woolf has called: "the humane art which owes its origin to the love of friends."

# Dorothy Osborne

1627-1695

IN 1836 Thomas Peregrine Courtenay published *Memoirs of the Life, Works and Correspondence of Sir William Temple.* Apologetically, in an appendix he added forty-two extracts from letters written to Temple by Dorothy Osborne during the two years before their marriage in 1654. In reviewing Courtenay's book in *The Edinburgh Review,* Thomas Babington Macaulay singled out these extracts as of particular value: "Mr. Courtenay expresses some doubt whether his readers will think him justified in inserting so large a number of these epistles. We only wish there were twice as many." Macaulay regarded them as of more historical value than ten times their weight in state papers taken at random:

> To us surely it is as useful to know how the young ladies of England employed themselves a hundred and eighty years ago, how far their minds were activated, what were their favorite studies, what degree of liberty was allowed to them, what use they made of that liberty, what accomplishments they most valued in men, and what proofs of tenderness delicacy permitted them to give favored suitors, as to know about the seizure of Franche Comte and the Treaty of Nimeguen. The mutual relations of the two sexes seem to us to be at least as important as the mutual relations of any two governments in the world; and a series of letters written by a virtuous, amiable and sensitive girl, and intended for the eyes of her lover alone, can scarcely fail to throw some light on the relation of the sexes.

The letters—they were not edited separately and published in full until 1888—do indeed throw plenty of light on the relation of the sexes, and historically they are the only firsthand account of the ordinary everyday life of the English aristocracy and gentry during the Protectorate of Oliver Cromwell. Yet their prime interest must always be a personal one; a vivid revelation of a particular young woman, gentle, reserved, courageous, battling with adverse circumstances and temperamental low spirits—" 'Tis not that I am sad . . . but I never appear to be very merry"—in a situation where she had ample reason for despondency:

> Can there be a more romance story than ours would make if the conclusion should prove happy? Ah! I dare not hope it. Something that I cannot describe draws a cloud over all the light my fancy discovers sometimes, and leaves me in the dark with all my fears about me.

Indeed the story was romantic. Lady Giffard, Temple's sister, later wrote an account of their first meeting. In 1647 young William Temple, then twenty, second son of Sir John Temple, Master of the Rolls in Dublin—though at this date suspended from his office—set out to complete his education with a tour of Europe. He stopped to see some cousins in the Isle of Wight, and at an inn in the same village he met the son and daughter of Sir Peter Osborne, also setting out abroad. Sir Peter had been courageously and obstinately holding Castle Cornet in Guernsey for the King since 1643, but after years of broken promises of reinforcements, and of spending his own money to provision his troops, he had recently resigned his command and was living in exile in St. Malo. Young Robin, his son, a staunch Royalist too, scratched an insult to the Roundheads on a window pane of the inn. For this their party was arrested and brought before the Governor. Dorothy Osborne, then twenty-one, relying on his chivalry, took the offense upon herself, which brought their release. Maybe Temple interceded with the Governor, who was also a cousin of his. Anyhow he fell in love with the spirited girl and she with him, and when they reached St. Malo, he stayed on to enjoy her company. Sir Peter Osborne, however, had been ruined by the war, and Sir John Temple's own fortunes were very uncertain. The match seemed totally unsuitable to both families, and Temple was ordered to continue his travels.

In 1649 Sir Peter and his family were permitted to return to his English estate, Chicksands Priory, near Campton, in Bedfordshire. (It still belongs to the Osborne family.) When relating to Temple later her feelings at the time, Dorothy describes the frayed state of her nerves:

> When I came out of France, nobody knew me again, I was so altered, from a cheerful humour that was always pleased, I was grown heavy and sullen, froward and discomposed.

Nor can her life have brought her much cheer. Chicksands, originally a fifteenth-century nunnery, confiscated by Henry VIII, had been the Osborne home for more than a hundred years. Sir Peter had been a wealthy man, but the war had impoverished him. His wife, who had had to spend her time visiting relatives with her children during his absence in Guernsey, was already ailing on his return and died two years later, assuring her daughter: "I have lived to see it is almost impossible to believe people worse than they are; and so will you." One of the sons had been killed in the war, and another, young Robin, was to die shortly afterwards. The eldest was married and lived in Gloucestershire, and the second, of whom we hear much in the letters, was a jealous bully and implacably hostile towards Temple, adding greatly to Dorothy's trials. Her sisters were married, and the responsibility for running the household and the entertainment of guests rested on her. The portrait of her as a girl shows a sad, thoughtful, rather long face, with large heavy-lidded dark eyes and hair. She looks intelligent rather than beautiful, and evidently gave the impression of austerity and aloofness. She asks Temple rather anxiously: "Do I look so stately as people apprehend?" and she evidently had none of the animation and striking good looks of her lover. The portrait of young William Temple by Sir Peter Lely, in the National Portrait Gallery in London, has luxuriant dark brown curling hair, gray eyes and a squarish face with clear-cut features, a hair-line moustache and great charm of expression. His sister said of him that he had "more spirit and life in him than ever I saw in anybody . . . and that he never had a mind to make anybody kind to him that he did not compass it."

Unfortunately Temple was kept traveling abroad so that he could not cheer or charm Dorothy. They had a short meeting in London in 1651, and she speaks later of having had a letter from Breda after that, but it was not until December 1652 that he wrote to tell her he was shortly to return to London, and her reply is the first time that we listen to her own voice. It was four years since their first meeting—she was now twenty-five and he a year younger. We do not know what he said, but they had evidently had a wager that she was to pay him ten pounds if she married during his absence, and he has asked if it is due. She tells him that it is not and that he had better regard it as a "desperate debt, for 'tis a very uncertain one." She is extremely glad to hear from him "since (without compliment) there are very few persons in the world I am more concerned in." But she is very cautious about any happy outcome:

> To find that you have overcome your long journey, that you are well and in a place where it is possible for me to see you, is such a satisfaction as I, who have not been used to many, may be allowed to doubt of.

Nevertheless, she hopes for another letter: "You know how to direct it, for I am where I was, still the same and always your humble servant, D. Osborne." They did not meet, however, until late in February. On her return to Chicksands, half-dead with a heavy cold and the fatigues of the journey, she writes: "I have only so much sense left as to wish you were here too. When that leaves me you may conclude me past all."

She signed this "Your affectionate friend and servant," and the tone of the letters suggests that they had pledged themselves to constancy. She is no longer cautious:

> You ask my thoughts but at one hour; you will think me bountiful, I hope, when I shall tell you I know no hour when you have them not. No, in earnest, my very dreams are yours, and I have got such a habit of thinking of you that any other thought intrudes and grows uneasy to me.

Letters were exchanged weekly. The carrier brought his on Thursdays and takes her replies back on Mondays. She gives him plenty of commissions to buy things for her in London. Hearing that seals are very much in fashions and that "such as are oldest and oddest are most prized," she urges him: "if such things come in your way, pray remember me." Apparently they often did, and one wonders what she did with the numbers that go to be "set" by Mr. Walker, the goldsmith. "Orange-flower water" is always welcome, and she would like what sounds like a case of scissors (French *étuis*):

> Did you not say once you knew where good French tweeses were to be had? Pray send me a pair; they shall cut no love.

They exchange volume after volume of French romances, and she would like a copy of Lady Newcastle's poetry:

> They say 'tis ten times more extravagant than her dress. Sure, the poor woman is a little distracted, she could never be so ridiculous else as to venture at writing books, and in verse too.

Temple's side of the correspondence has not survived, but hers pictures her daily life, her family and friends, her opinions and her emotions, as well as the social gossip of her environment, for the nearly two years of uncertainty and deferred hopes before the reluctant families would give consent to the marriage. We know nothing of Dorothy's education, but she was a born writer, mingling easily the tones of gossip, reflection, humor, affectionate reserve or black misery. She had very definite ideas of what writing should be: "All letters, methinks, should be free and easy as one's discourse, not studied as an oration, nor made up of hard words like a charm." Nothing should "obscure the plain sense," nothing stilted or artificial. She reflects the speaking voice so vividly as she rallies him roundly about his pessimism:

> I have said anything that came into my head to put you out of your dumps. For God's sake be in better humour, and assure yourself I am as much as you can wish, your Faithful Friend and servant.

When he evidently remonstrated about this form of signature, she can only say: "Love is a terrible word, and I should blush to death if anything but a letter accused me of it."

They are lovers, however, though star-crossed ones. Their families are busy all this time trying to arrange more advantageous matches for them both. Dorothy was probably glad that Temple should know of her many "servants." In her third letter, catching up on the news during his long absence, she tells of five suitors she has had, and later reports a scene with her jealous brother where "all the people I had ever in my life refused were brought again upon the stage, like Richard III's ghosts, to reproach me withal." They range from a pompous middle-aged widower with four unmarried daughters, "the vainest, impertinent, self-conceited, learned coxcomb that you ever saw," whose letters are "the most sublime nonsense," to a shy youth who cannot come to the point: "In my life, I never heard a man say more, nor less to the purpose." But the most favored of her beaux seems strangely to have been Henry Cromwell, second son of the Protector, who sends her "two of the finest young Irish greyhounds that ever I saw."

It is true that Henry did not take after the rest of the family, and was labeled "a debauched, ungodly cavalier" by a Puritan commentator, but it is surprising that a daughter of the passionate royalist, Sir Peter Osborne, should ever meet, much less be wooed by a Cromwell. But it is interesting to note from the letters how soon after the end of the Civil War, families whose sons and brothers had fought and died on opposite sides of the conflict settled down amicably to exchange visits, to intermarry and to return to normal social relationships—life in general does not seem to have been revolutionized in any way for the aristocracy. In spite of the Puritan victory, they continue to have race-meetings and masques, to frequent fashionable spas where they "go abroad all day and play [gamble] all night," to have large noisy country houseparties and stage private theatricals. Dorothy has difficulty in not laughing when she goes to hear a radical preacher in their village church, who tells the astonished countryfolk "some forty times" that "if there were no kings, no queens, no lords and ladies, nor gentlemen, nor gentlewomen, in the world, 'twould be no loss at all to God Almighty."

But life at Chicksands was not gay. Her father became a complete invalid and never left his room. In a much quoted letter Dorothy describes a typical fine summer day. What must a wet or wintry one have been!

> You ask me how I pass my time here. I can give you a perfect account not only of what I do for the present, but what I am likely to do this seven years if I stay here so long. I rise in the morning reasonably early and before I am ready I go round the house till I am weary of that, and then into the garden till it grows too hot for me. About ten o'clock I think of making me ready, and when that's done, I go into my father's chamber, from thence to dinner, where my cousin Molle and I sit in great state in a room and at a table that would hold a great many more. After dinner we sit and talk till Mr. B. comes in question, and then I am gone. The heat of the day is spent in reading or working, and about six or seven o'clock I walk out into a common that lies hard by the house, where a great many young wenches keep sheep and cows and sit in the shade singing of ballads . . . I talk to them, and find they want nothing to make them the happiest people in the world

> but the knowledge that they are so. . . . When I see them driving home their cattle, I think 'tis time for me to retire too. When I have supped, I go into the garden, and so to the side of a small river that runs by it, when I sit down and wish you with me. . . . I sit there sometimes till I am lost with thinking . . .

Cousin Molle was a Fellow of King's College, Cambridge, and not a welcome visitor, as his chief concern was his health. He also always pressed the suit of his friend Mr. B. in whom Dorothy had no interest. On one occasion he begs a picture of Dorothy for him:

> But, I thank God, an imagination took him one morning that he was falling into a dropsy, and made him in such haste to go back to Cambridge to his doctor, that he never remembered anything he had to ask of me, but the coach to carry him away.

Another boring relative was the garrulous Widow Thorold. To avoid listening "woodenly" to her chatter, Dorothy arranges card games and sees to it that the widow wins. In the middle of one game a letter from Temple arrives. Dorothy makes an excuse that she must fetch some more cash from her room, and "took time enough to have coined myself some money if I had had the art of it," while she reads the letter. But her greatest trials are the visits of her brother Henry, and she is hard put to it to be humorous about *him*. She speaks of his "persecution" of her, and his jealousy of Temple and fury at Dorothy's constancy seem to support her own hint that there is something perverted in his feeling for her:

> Seriously, I many times receive letters from him, that were they seen without any address to me or his name, nobody would believe they were from a brother; and I cannot but tell him sometimes that, sure, he mistakes and sends me letters meant for his mistress.

He brings gossip not only of Temple's poverty, but of his "want of honour and religion," and his unprincipled efforts at self-advancement. It makes Dorothy lose her reserve:

> I forgot all my disguise, and we talked ourselves weary; he renounced me again, and I defied him, but both in as civil language as it would permit, and parted in great anger with the usual ceremony of a leg and a curtsey, that you would have died with laughing to have seen us.

The next evening, however, they lose their anger in a talk on religion, and ask pardon of each other: "Two hermits conversing in a cell . . . never expressed more humble, charitable kindness, one towards the other, than we." Henry promises a truce, but declares he can never see her again if the marriage takes place:

> Not out of want of kindness to me, but because he cannot see the ruin of a person he loves so passionately, and in whose happiness he has laid up all his.

He continued to "bait" her, however, and it is no wonder that when the "treaty" of marriage was finally to be settled, Temple's father objected to Henry as the representative of her family. Dorothy overpersuaded Sir John, but three days before the ceremony, Henry broke off negotiations. The marriage went forward, and Dorothy and Temple brought suit against him for withholding her dowry. It was not until seven months later that a settlement was made. We do not know if they ever met again, but Henry died unmarried in 1675.

Life at Chicksands was very dull, but though Dorothy declares that Temple's love "makes all the happiness I have or ever shall be capable of," her letters give us plenty of material on "the relation of the sexes" among other couples in the aristocracy and gentry. Her reports and opinions are of course colored by her own high ideals of class and conduct. She is quite disillusioned about the average marriage. Of her brother and his wife she comments: "He loves her, I think, at the ordinary rate of husbands," but there are a great many ordinary types of husband that will not do for *her*. She sketches various of them to Temple: the country gentleman who understands nothing but hawks and dogs, and prefers them to his wife; the one who reads no books and knows nothing but a few Latin tags; the narrowly educated who never gets beyond book-learning; the town gallant who must always have company; the traveled Monsieur "whose head is all feather inside and outside, and can talk of nothing but dancing and duels." In fact, her husband must have had "that kind of breeding that I have had, and used that kind of company."

The breeding is very strict in matters of the heart. In spite of her delight in the interminable French romances, which seem to make most of her reading, they sometimes shock her. The young women in them are too forward.

> It will never enter my head that 'tis possible any woman can love where she is not first loved, and much less that if they should do that, they could have the face to own it.

Yet where love is mutual, she sees no distinction between the sexes. Friendship, she insists, "is wholly governed by equality, and can there be such a thing in it as a distinction of power? . . . Indeed a mistress and a servant sounds otherwise, but that is ceremony, and this is truth." But at a houseparty of realistic young people she finds her romantic ideals are made fun of: "I cannot beat into their heads a passion that must be subject to no decay . . . all this is perfect nonsense in their opinion." Not only do they not see this "truth," but the lack of "ceremony," both among single and married women horrifies her. She sees a letter from a young woman just engaged: "She is absolutely wild with joy as anything in Bedlam is mad, and all that she says is so strangely disjointed that one who did not know her would think she were a very odd body." A young wife kissing her husband "in the midst of all the company," seems to her "very rude"; on the other side, however, is the shocking behaviour of Lady Sandys, who went to the Winchester race meeting with Colonel Paunton. The lady unexpectedly met her husband there and refused to go home with him. Or there is the sad case of Lady Anne Blunt, who has made a runaway match and "is the talk of all the footmen and boys in the street, and will be company for them shortly."

The open pursuit of rich widows causes her a lot of cynical amusement, and she is amazed at the way young people rush into marriage "as inconsiderately as a woodcock runs into a noose," and are carried by the weakest considerations imaginable "to do a thing of the greatest consequence of anything that concerns this world." Like many people before and since, Dorothy is sure her own times are peculiar in all this:

> What an age we live in, when 'tis a miracle if in ten couple that are married, two of them live so as not to publish to the world that they cannot agree.

She blames the women for this, having observed that "generally in great families, the men seldom disagree, but the women are always scolding." Yet she finds one excuse for the follies of the young people of the day; it is that "the want of a Court to govern themselves by is in great part the cause of their ruin." There, at least external conformity to social rules was demanded, and since "there are not many that are sober enough to be trusted with the government of themselves," it is safer to be ruled by a conventional authority.

Dorothy can laugh at her own sensitivity about her clandestine relation to Temple, and wishes she could refrain from blushing when his name is mentioned, since "a blush is the foolishest thing that can be, and betrays one more than a red nose does a drunkard." She can also be more tolerant than some of her moralizing suggests. She agrees that the second marriage of Lady Sunderland to a Mr. Smith belies her reputation for wit and discretion, but she adds: "We are all mortal." However, as far as she herself is concerned, she is adamant about propriety and decorum and suitable marriage settlements. If these can be satisfactory, "all the advantages of fortune or person imaginable met together in one man should not be preferred before you." Yet marriage is a social and family institution and its "ceremony" must be observed: "I can never think of disposing myself without my father's consent . . . 'Tis my duty. . . . Nor could you like it in me if I should do otherwise, 'twould make me unworthy of your esteem." In the same way, she says she would hate herself if she caused any "disorder" between Temple and *his* father. She is also morbidly afraid of what people would say of her if she rashly married for love. Can he remember any who have done so and not repented it, she challenges him, and "is there anything thought so indiscreet or that makes one more contemptible?" To his suggestion that her fears are founded on vanity she can only reply:

> Possibly it is a weakness in me to aim at the world's esteem. . . . But there are certain things that custom has made almost of absolute necessity, and reputation I take to be one of them.

Dorothy's opinions were no doubt founded on much observation and knowledge of her world, and of the helplessness and vulnerability of women in it, but they sprang also from a temperamental lack of self-confidence and a deep-seated distrust of life: "I find so many things to fear and so few to hope." Even in the early days of the correspondence, in spite of her shafts of wit and her companionable charm, the undercurrent of sadness is always there:

> I do not know that I ever desired anything earnestly in my life but 'twas denied me; I am many times afraid to wish a thing, merely lest my fortune should take that occasion to use me ill.

When Temple rallies her and declares that he can "fancy a perfect happiness," she replies: "that is not much, many people do so; but I never heard of anyone that had it more than in fancy"; and declares that their situation is "a common calamity," which must be endured. She can think of no reason why so many young people are denied the satisfaction of pleasing themselves in marriage "but that it is a happiness too great for this world and might endanger our forgetting the next."

When the letters start Dorothy is already under medical treatment for the Spleen, that fashionable disorder of the seventeenth and eighteenth centuries which seems to cover everything which in our day is attributed to "stress." Temple himself in his later essay on *Health and Long Life* gives an excellent description of symptoms familiar to us all, and brings home how frustration, anxiety, guilt, and emotional repressions were as prevalent and as disastrous to health in Dorothy's day as in our own:

> Whatever the Spleen is; whether a disease of the part so called, or of people that ail something, but they know not what: it is certainly a very ill ingredient into any other disease. . . . For as hope is the sovereign balsam of life, and the best cordial in all distempers both of body or mind; so fear, and regret, and melancholy apprehensions, which are the usual effects of the Spleen . . . are the worst accidents that can attend any disease. . . . 'Tis no matter what is made the occasion . . . a disappointed hope, a blot of honour, a strain of conscience, an unfortunate love, an aching jealousy, a repining grief, will serve the turn.
>
> I remember an ingenious physician who told me . . . he found most of his patients so disturbed by troubles of conscience, that he was forced to play the divine with them, before he could begin the physician.

Dorothy visited Epsom to drink the waters, and at home took a cup of "infusion of steel" in white wine daily. She tells her lover: "I drink your health every morning in a drench that would poison a horse I believe, and 'tis the only way I have to persuade myself to take it." She has little faith in the prescription, but is frightened by stories of what the Spleen will do: "They tell me 'twill not leave me common sense, that I shall hardly be fit company for my own dogs, and that it will end either in a stupidness . . . or fill my head with such whims as will make me ridiculous."

In spite of her precautions, however, the nervous strain of her emotional situation proved too much for her. Nursing her dying father, ever on guard against her jealous brother, who tried to intercept Temple's letters, and threw scene after scene of anger and tears, fending off suitor after suitor pressed on her by her family—all this built up a mounting tension, and in the late summer of 1653, it is clear that the tension had affected Temple too. "Why are you so sullen, and why am I the cause?" she complains to him: "Good God! how are you altered; and what is it that has done it?" It was first of all her own vacillation about coming to London, which had to depend on the plans of others; then, when in October she did go, the visit was clearly not a success. Her brother came with her for one thing, and something else seems to have planted a distrust of one another as well as of fortune, in the place of their staunch faith. It sent Dorothy into a pathological depression. She had reached breaking point, and for the next two months all her usual quiet sadness and quiet humor and quiet devotion turned to bitter emotional conflict and to despair. By November 13 she is writing that her "long strife with herself" has brought her to the conviction that her love has been a sin: "it was guilty in being greater than is allowable for things of this world"; it was "but a refined degree of madness," and must be renounced. She sees it as the ruin of them both, and for herself wants nothing but to give up the struggle against it:

> I have no ends nor no designs, nor will my heart ever be capable of any; but like a country wasted by a civil war, where two opposing parties have disputed their right so long till they have made it worth neither of their conquests, 'tis ruined and desolated by the long strife within it to that degree as 'twill be useful to none.

She wants nothing but "an early and a quiet grave, free from the trouble of this busy world."

Her emotional exhaustion even produces a petulance and self-pity we have never heard in her voice before. To Temple's insistence that he must come and see her she gives a chillingly egotistical answer:

> You may do so if you please, though I know not to what end. You deceive yourself if you think it would prevail upon me to alter my intentions; besides, I can make no contrivances; it must be here, and I must endure the noise it will make, and undergo the censures of a people that choose ever to give the worst interpretation that anything will bear. Yet if it can be any ease to you to make me more miserable than I am, never spare me; consider yourself only, and me not at all.

Temple evidently had the wisdom not to cross her wishes, and it is clear that she passed into a phase of emotional withdrawal, a "strange insensibility." Her misfortunes, she says, "have taken away all sense of everything else from me, and left me a walking misery only." Again she takes refuge in the assurance that it is God's will; He would have decreed otherwise had He intended them to be happy.

It must have encouraged Temple considerably, however, that in this same letter she speaks of the impossibility of their meeting as mere friends: "To deal freely with you, that were to betray myself, and I find that my passion would quickly be my master again if I gave it any liberty." Temple's reply to this must have cleared up the original cause of her emotional collapse, and in the next letter she is herself again and takes back all her despairing self-dramatizations:

> I must tell you that, unless it were after the receipt of those letters that made me angry, I never had the least hope of wearing out my passion, nor, to say truth, much desire.

"We'll have no more quarrels," she promises, "no more fears, no more jealousies," and she pledges herself to him irrevocably. Within a few weeks Temple paid a hurried visit to Chicksands and they had a few stolen hours together. For once, Dorothy consents to prevaricate with her brother and "tell a great lie." For the sake of peace and "to keep him from playing the madman" she declares that Temple had come to make a formal leave-taking before going abroad. It was only half a lie, since a plan was already made that Temple should join his father in Dublin, where Sir John had just been reappointed Master of the Rolls. But Henry would certainly have played the madman if he had read of Dorothy's request to her lover at the end of this letter: "Before you go I must have a ring from you, a plain gold one: if I ever marry it shall be my wedding ring."

Although Dorothy's faith in Temple's love was now utterly secure, her troubles were far from over. The ring came, and a lock of hair, and fresh hopes that Sir John's new office might bring some opening in government service for his son. There was talk of a post in the Embassy in Sweden, but it fell through, and in March 1654 Sir Peter Osborne died, leaving Dorothy "in the condition (which of all others) is the most insupportable to my nature, to depend upon kindred that are not friends." Her brother, to whom she rashly owned her secret engagement, revenged himself by spreading malicious gossip about Temple, and about her own headstrong folly. She hoped to stay on at Chicksands, but was sent off on visits to relations, first in London and then in Kent. Temple's own agitation and ardor speak in the one letter of his that has survived:

> How hard it is to think of ending when I am writing to you; but it must be so, and I must ever be subject to other people's occasions . . . both in respect of this fellow's post that is howling at me for my letters and of my father's delays. They kill me . . . yet you may command me over at one minute's warning. . . . For God's sake let me know of all your motions, when and where I may hope to see you . . . My dearest dear, adieu.

Dorothy replies urging obedience to his father's wishes, but owns her own situation is wretched, having to write "with the company prating about me, and some of them so bent on doing me little mischiefs."

She longs for the quiet of Chicksands, but has no privacy and has to join in the general social life about her. She dines at fashionable taverns, goes masked with a party to Spring Gardens and has her portrait painted by a famous miniaturist, Samuel Cooper. She finds it all very boring and her companions very empty-headed, and apparently tells them so, which would hardly maker her popular—as she very well knows: "Fie! I am got into my complaining humour that tires myself as well as everybody else, and which (as you observe) helps not at all." It is no better when she moves in July to the house of her brother-in-law and his second wife in the country: "so strangely crowded with company that I am weary as a dog already, though I have been here but three or four days." It is "a house the most filled of any since the Ark." When there seems room for no more they are joined by two colonels, "the greatest drinkers that ever I saw." They all sit up till three o'clock in the morning and then Dorothy has to share her bed with two other girls. To make matters worse, her brother-in-law, outraged by his wife's over-hospitable tastes, wrangles and finds fault with her all day long. Dorothy finally bursts out: "I would not live thus a twelve-month to gain all that the King has lost, unless it were to give it to him again."

Luckily, by the end of September, Temple was back in London, with his father's consent to go forward with the marriage "treaty." Dorothy joined him in October to make final preparations for the wedding. Happy little notes replace the long letters.

> You are like to have an excellent housewife of me; I am abed still, and slept so soundly, nothing but your letter could have waked me. You shall hear from me as soon as we have dined. Farewell: can you endure that word? No, out upon't—I'll see you anon.

Or when she disappoints him of her company:

> I cannot call on you tonight—am engaged to sup and play. Poor man, I am sorry for you: in earnest, I shall be quite spoiled. . . . Think whether it were not best to leave me and begin a new adventure.

But tragedy struck again. On November 9, a week before they were to be married, Dorothy fell ill of the smallpox, and nearly died. Her beauty was marred, but we can imagine that Temple could give his "dearest dear" assurances that his love for her was more than skin deep. As soon as she recovered, they were married on Christmas Day 1654.

Dorothy lived forty-one years longer, but we never have more than glimpses of her as wife and mother. For a year or two after marriage, they seem to have lived with relations of Temple at Reading, and it was there that her eldest son John was born in December 1655. In the few notes, apparently written to her husband during his absences in London, Dorothy gives us some of her old flashes of gaiety and new expressions of tender affection which she held in check before marriage. "I infinitely love my dearest dear heart" she assures him, and that he need not be afraid that the baby will supplant him in her devotion:

> 'Tis the quietest best little boy ever was born, I'm afraid he'll make me grow fond of him do what I can. The only way to keep me from it is for you to keep at home, for then I am less with him.

This makes sad reading when we know what the future had in store for her. She bore nine children, seven of whom died in infancy. The adored little daughter, Diana, ravishingly pretty in her portrait, died of smallpox when she was fourteen, and "the quietest, best little boy" seems to have inherited his mother's oversensitive nervous temperament. He grew to manhood, worked at the British Embassy in Paris, married a rich French girl and seemed headed to carry on his father's career in diplomacy. William III appointed him Secretary at War when he was thirty-two. Within a week of his appointment, however, apparently despairing because his first act in office had proved to be an error of judgment, he drowned himself in the Thames, leaving a farewell note:

> My folly in undertaking what I was not able to perform has done the King and the Kingdom a great deal of prejudice. I wish him all happiness and abler servants than John Temple.

The note still exists, with Dorothy's superscription: "Child's paper that he writ before he killed himself." To a nephew's letter of condolence she replied with some of her old sense of guilt and the need for submission:

> I give you many thanks for your kind letter and the sense you have of my affliction, which truly is very great. But since it is laid upon me by the hand of an Almighty and Gracious God, that always proportions His punishments to the support He gives with them, I may hope to bear it as a Christian ought to do, and more especially one that is conscious to herself of having many ways deserved it. The strange revolutions we have seen might well have taught me what this world is, yet it seems it was necessary that I should have a near example of the uncertainty of all human blessings, that so having no tie to the world I may the better prepare myself to leave it.

By then, 1689, the Temples were at Moor Park, near Farnham, in Surrey, where they had retired after various diplomatic missions and ambassadorial appointments in France, Brussels and The Hague, and the various ups and downs of political favoritism at home. Charles II created William a baronet, though not a peer, as his friends hoped, and he twice refused the position of Secretary of State, though he accepted an appointment to the Privy Council in 1679. His open criticism of Charles II for dissovling Parliament without consulting the Council caused him the loss of his office, and he sent a message to the King "that he would pass his life as good a subject as any in his Kingdom, but would never again meddle in public affairs." He devoted himself to writing his essays, editing his letters and memoirs, to riding and walking, to beautifying his house and tending his beloved fruit trees and shrubs and herb garden.

Young Jonathan Swift, as Sir William's secretary, shared their home during the last years. In a poem on Temple's recovery from an illness, Swift writes of "Mild Dorothea, peaceful, wise and great. . . . The best companion for the best of men." Alas, we have no comments by Dorothy on Swift, or on any of the subjects we should like to know her feelings about in later life. We know she was "so highly regarded in Holland . . . that it was usually said she wrote most of Sir William's letters." She was the valued friend and confidante of Queen Mary, wife of William III, both of whom they had known intimately as Prince and Princess of Orange in their years at the Hague. Lady Giffard, Temple's sister, called her "a very remarkable woman" and says she fitted into the Temple family "as naturally as if she had been born there." But what, one wonders, did Dorothy really feel about the perpetual presence of the very dominating Lady Giffard, who, having lost her husband two weeks after her marriage in 1661, made her home with the Temples during the rest of their lives? What did she feel about Temple himself, as he hardened into ultraconservatism and self-complacency? Did she always know of his manners with men, as reported by a young diplomat as early as 1677?

> He held me in discourse a great long hour, of things most relating to himself, which are never without vanity; but this most especially full of it, and some stories of his amours, and extraordinary abilities that way . . .

The picture is carried on by Swift in his *Resolutions when I come to be old,* jotted down just after Temple's death in 1699:

> Not to keep young company unless they really desire it.
> Not to be peevish or morose or suspicious.
> Not to be over severe with young people.
> Not to be too free of advice.
> Not to talk much or of myself.
> Not to boast of my former beauty, or strength, or favour with ladies etc.

Perhaps all these weaknesses increased when he had lost Dorothy's companionship, and her peace and wisdom, for she had died five years before.

# Jonathan Swift

1667-1745

ADDISON called Swift "the most agreeable companion, the truest friend and the greatest genius of his age." Here we can say very little about his genius or his relations with so many of the great men of his time in literature and in public life. His letters to these and to his personal men friends fill many volumes, but we cannot even touch those. Our subject is Swift's relations with the two women who created the private drama of his life, and the letters which form the basis for any judgment of those relationships.

Addison does not add to his description of Swift that he was the most baffling and mysterious figure of his age. In his public life in England he probably did not appear so. His friends and enemies knew him as the brilliant pamphleteer and savage satirist; his friends knew that he combined this with a warm geniality of spirit and unswerving personal loyalties. They must have known too that all his ambition for eminence in the Church or political diplomacy had been nipped, that he regarded the Deanery of St. Patrick's Cathedral as exile, and that he became a bitterly disappointed and disillusioned man. In Dublin, however, all the questions we now ask were asked in his lifetime, and were the subject of common gossip. Who was Esther Johnson, who came to be called Stella? What were her relations with Swift? Did they marry, and if not, why not, since his devotion to her was so clear? Were he and Hester Van Homrigh, whom he called Vanessa, lovers in the full sense of the term? Did they have a child? What were Swift's real feelings towards her? What happened just before her death which made her want to have their correspondence published as soon as she died? All these riddles must have been bandied about in what Swift called "the tattle of this nasty town." They gave rise to stories which were handed down at many removes, so that after Swift's death, his early biographers had, in addition to the letters called *The Journal to Stella* and Swift's memoir of Stella written after her death, and the correspondence with Vanessa, a store of legends and scraps of gossip which had accumulated round the secret drama, and could be interpreted according to the taste of the writer. But of direct factual evidence nothing conclusive has ever come to light, and we must still interpret subjectively, with the letters themselves as the only firm basis for opinion.

The mystery starts with the man himself. Who was Jonathan Swift? Of his birth and early childhood we know nothing at all except what he himself chose to tell in the fragment of autobiography found among his papers after his death. No record of his birth or baptism exists in Dublin, or of his alleged father's death. He simply tells us that he was a posthumous child and follows this with a story of being kidnaped by his nurse as an infant and spending years with her in England, until he returned to Dublin and was adopted by an uncle, Godwin Swift, and sent to school and then to Trinity College. The researches of Denis Johnston, in his book *In Search of Swift* leave us with another barrage of questions. If his father was the poor law clerk whose name he bore, how did he come to be married by special license, which cost money? And how could he settle twenty pounds a year in *English* funds upon his widow? If he was adopted by his uncle Godwin, how did he come to have a more expensive education than Godwin's own sons? Why, when in his own words he was "stopped of his degree for dullness and insufficiency," and by the College records, his behaviour seems to have been as unsatisfactory as his scholarship—why did he have such a degree granted "by special grace"? Finally, when he left College at the age of twenty-two, and went to join his mother in Leicester, why did she advise him to apply to Sir William Temple for employment?

Mr. Johnston is very persuasive in arguing that these and many other points all suggest that Swift was the natural son of Sir John Temple, William's father. At the time of Swift's birth, Sir John was a widower and Master of the Rolls in Dublin. He died in 1677 when Swift was ten years old, but as his will was not made public and is now lost, nothing can be proved from that. Swift's own account of his birth and early days is certainly suspect, but the theory of his paternity has finally to rest on a series of suppositions.

Swift came to the Temples' in 1689, a few months after the death of their son. Temple said of the arrangement: "His whole family having long been known to me obliged me . . . to take care of him." Nowadays, Moor Park is more famous because Swift lived there on and off for ten years than because it was the home of Sir William Temple. And the woman with whom it is associated is not Dorothy Temple or the self-important Lady Giffard, but Esther Johnson, daughter of Lady Giffard's widowed housekeeper. Swift was no doubt of the greatest value to Temple, who needed a competent secretary to deal with his still large political correspondence and to prepare his papers and writings for future publication. But Swift too must have benefited enormously from the association. No doubt, Temple was often difficult and moody; Swift reminds Stella years later: "Don't you remember how I used to be in pain when Sir William Temple would look cold and out of humour for three or four days, and I used to suspect a hundred reasons?" No doubt the proud, raw youth continually felt humiliated by his dependent position and lack of social graces, but probably he owed the ease of his acceptance later into the highest social and intellectual circles, to the training in culture and elegance that the Temple household gave him, as well as to the training and insight it gave him in public affairs. Moreover he had enough leisure to practice and discipline his own burgeoning creative gifts, and though Swift's writing developed a strength and breadth and vitality far beyond Temple's elegance and ease, at the age of twenty-five Swift wrote that he preferred Temple's style "to all others at present in English."

In 1694, as Temple showed no signs of using his influence to promote his own career, Swift, against Temple's wish, took orders and was given a small living in northern Ireland. Beyond falling in love with Jane Waring, whom he called Varina, daughter of an archdeacon, his life was completely uneventful. Varina refused his offer of marriage, and the episode is of interest only as rather strong evidence that Swift was not impotent, as some critics argue. His letters to her are very warm in praise of the physical joys of love. Less than two years later, Swift was glad to accept Temple's offer to return to Moor Park.

Esther Johnson was then fifteen and evidently a great favorite with Temple. Later in life it was freely affirmed that she was Temple's natural daughter. If this were true, and if, as Denis Johnston believes, Swift and Temple were half-brothers, that would offer a convincing obstacle to marriage between them. But again all the evidence is hearsay. Temple's known fondness for children, and the loss of his own beloved daughter, would be reason enough for his interest in the attractive child, and for the fact that he left her a little money and property in his will. What is certain is that a very strong bond of affection developed between her and Swift. He was fourteen years older than Stella and acted as her tutor as well as friend. As he wrote thirty years later to one of his men friends, when she was dying: "This was a person of my own rearing and instruction from childhood, who excelled in every good quality that can possibly accomplish a human creature." Another lowly member of the household was Rebecca Dingley, an older poor relation of the Temples, whom Lady Giffard evidently exploited when she was in need of domestic help.

All this settled comfortable existence came to an end with Temple's death in 1699. He left Swift a hundred pounds and the tiresome duties of literary executor, but had taken no steps to forward his career in literature or politics or the Church. It was always Swift's fate to be of such service to his patrons that they would do nothing to advance him elsewhere. All he could get was the living of Laracor, a village about twenty miles from Dublin, where again he took up the life of a country clergyman. But he was also made a Prebend in St. Patrick's Cathedral and became active in the affairs of the Irish Church. Two years later, on a visit to London on Church business, he persuaded Stella, then just turned twenty, to leave her mother, and with Rebecca Dingley, to make her home near him. Swift admits, in his Memoir of Stella, written twenty-five years later, that the curious relationship caused talk:

> The adventure looked so like a frolic, the censure held for some time, as if there were a secret history in such a removal, which however soon blew off by her excellent conduct.

Indeed they always practiced an exaggerated propriety. The ladies lodged in the nearby town of Trim, or in Dublin, but during Swift's absences would sometimes move to the parsonage, or later, to the Deanery. Several commentators noted that Swift was never *known* to meet Stella except in the presence of a third person.

A new actor appeared shortly: the Reverend William Tisdall, who wished to marry Stella. After a suit of several years, he wrote to Swift in 1704, evidently inquiring about Swift's own intentions toward her. Swift replied courteously:

> First, if my fortunes and humour served me to think of that state I should certainly among all persons on earth, make your choice; because I never saw that person whose conversation I entirely valued but hers. . . . And secondly I must assure you sincerely that this regard of mine never once entered into my head to be an impediment to you.

There are those who think that Stella kept Mr. Tisdall dangling to see if a rival would provoke Swift into declaring his own feelings. Yet it is difficult not to believe from the tone of the later *Journal*, that throughout their emotional relationship was based on full understanding and entire confidence, and that whatever the impediment was to their marriage Stella knew it and accepted it.

So the situation molded itself for ten years into the established and loving intimacy which is created in the so-called *Journal to Stella*. As a matter of fact, the first time Swift addressed Esther Johnson as Stella was in some birthday verses in 1718, when she was thirty-seven, and we don't know how or when he began to call her that. The letters were given the title by Thomas Sheridan in his edition of Swift's writings published in 1784.

These sixty-five letters to her and Rebecca Dingley, for he always pretends to be addressing them both, were written between September 1710 and June 1713. Swift was sent again to London on Church business, expecting to stay a few months and stayed nearly three years. Stella's side of the correspondence is all lost. Presumably Swift destroyed it all before his death. The letters were published in two batches. The first forty were edited by Swift's cousin—with the confusing name of Deane Swift—a most unscrupulous editor, who burnt all the originals and tampered with the text. He substituted "Stella" for the letters "ppt" (probably "poppet") and replaced "pdfr" (possibly "poor dear foolish rogue") by "Presto," a name given later to Swift by the Duchess of Shrewsbury. However, the last twenty-five letters had been published two years earlier, in 1766, unmutilated, by John Hawkesworth, and the originals of these are now in the British Museum. There we can see the faded, discolored sheets, crowded to the edges with the small, neat writing; the abbreviations and the blots—one with the comment: "Is that tobacco on the top of the paper, or what? I don't remember I slobbered." And the strange "little language," whose function and origin is still a mystery. This is a vocabulary of more than a hundred words, formed by substituting one letter for another or certain consonantal sounds for one another: "our richer gangridge" stands for "our little language," or "deelest sollars bose" for "dearest sirrahs both." Scholars are disinclined to relate it to Stella's childhood speech, since she was already eight years old when Swift first met her. Maybe it was some sort of joking cypher they evolved in early days, which became a symbol of their close intimacy.

The "little language," however, is of importance only as an illustration of that intimacy. In the letters Swift leaves the company of the statesmen and courtiers and men of letters he was living among; he leaves the purely masculine world of his writing, so virile, so concentrated, so full of satiric savagery and battering arguments—he leaves all this to be in as close contact as possible with two women living in the cramping society of a few of the minor clergy and of the genteel petty bourgeoisie of Dublin. During these years, Swift rose to be one of the most powerful influences in English politics; the close friend and adviser of the Tory government, headed by Robert Harley (later Lord Oxford), the Lord Treasurer, and Henry St. John (later Viscount Bolingbroke) Secretary of State. He was the most brilliant of their journalists and lampooners, the most feared by the Whigs. He dined and supped with dukes and duchesses, diplomats and ministers of state; he was welcome at all meetings of wits and scholars; he was plagued to help all his needy friends and by a host of place-hunters, often strangers. Yet this extraordinary man seldom went to bed at night or out in the morning without taking out his large sheet of paper (stolen from the office of the Lord Secretary) and establishing contact with his "dear rogues," his "little monkeys mine," his dear, saucy brats or sluts: "I will write something every day to MD (probably "my dears") and make it a sort of journal . . . and I shall always be in conversation with MD and MD with Presto."

It is real talking: "all the while I was undressing myself there I was speaking monkey things in air, just as if MD had been by"; and later: "so be quiet till I am gone to bed, then sit down by me a little and we'll talk a few words more." Or he will pretend that Stella is playing at being "a wheedling slut" and won't let him stop writing: "I can nor will stay any longer now: no I won't . . . no, no, look off, don't smile at me and say Pray, pray, Presto, write a little more." Stella's own letters become personified:

> And now let us see what this saucy dear letter of MD says. Come out letter, come out from between the sheets. . . . Hold up your head, like a good letter.

Their news, as he comments on it, sounds dull enough. Gossip about Dublin friends and the births and deaths in their small circle; the household expenses; their evenings at cards; their visits to Wexford to drink the waters. They ask him to send them things from London: a roll of tobacco to make Dingley's snuff, a pair of "hinged spectacles" for her; a green silk apron for Stella and tea, chocolate, salad plates, "palsy water" are all requested. Stella is a poor speller and Swift collects examples of her mistakes and jokes about her ignorance of the Bible and of politics. As to concrete pictures of them, Swift supplies his own humorous, teasing dramatizations. He is always urging them to take exercise:

> If I was with you, I'd make you walk. . . . Stella is naturally a stout walker and carries herself firm, methinks I see her strut and step clean over a kennel; and Dingley will do well enough if her petticoats were pinned up, but she is so embroiled and so fearful, and then Stella scolds and Dingley stumbles and is so daggled.

He knows exactly the mistakes that made Stella lose four shillings and eightpence at ombre with her "gang of deans":

> Would any but a mad lady go out twice upon Manilo, Basto and two small diamonds? Then in that game of spades, you

blundered when you had ten-ace; I never saw the like of you: and now you are in a huff because I tell you this.

This affectionate banter holds throughout: "Fig for your physician and his advice, Madam Dingley . . . your fall of the leaf; what care I when the leaves fall? I am sorry to see them fall with all my heart; but why should I take physic because the leaves fall off the trees?" They exchange bad puns, nor is he at all afraid of an off-color joke or a sexual innuendo:

> I was brought privately to Mr. Harley . . . he has appointed me an hour on Saturday . . . when I will open my business to him; which expression I would not use if I were a woman. I know you smoked it; but I did not till I writ it.

Another morning he must hurry out on political business:

> So I cannot stay fiddling and talking with dear little brats . . . 'tis still terribly cold—I wish my cold hand was in the warmest place about you, young women, I'd give ten guineas upon that account with all my heart, faith; oh, it starves my thigh.

The talk always comes back to the feeling of loving companionship which writing to them creates in him. The letters end with extravagant explosions of affection: "Presto loves MD infinitely above all earthly things," or "more than his life a thousand million of times." He finds "peace and quiet with MD and nowhere else," and he prays twice a day that they may all be happy together again, for "MD's felicity is the great end I aim at in all my pursuits."

Month after month, and then year after year, we listen to him talking about his daily problems. His nightcaps wear out: "I know not how to get others. I want a necessary woman strangely; I am as helpless as an elephant." His lodgings are very cold, but "cold or no cold" he won't start fires before November 1st or have them after April 1st. Economy is always very much to the fore: the thought of having to give Christmas tips haunts him and "slobbery weather" means coach or chair hire every time he goes out to dinner. But when spring comes he thinks of Laracor and his "canal" with its willows, and trout and eel fishing, and Stella riding by as he works in the garden. He moves his own lodgings to Chelsea, and the hayfields smell sweet as he walks from there to the city, and in the evenings he goes for a swim in the river, while "that rogue Patrick" holds his clothes on the bank.

Patrick, whom he brought from Ireland, is "an intolerable rascal." He drinks, gets into fights, forgets to light the fire, brings his master's gown and periwig so late that he misses an appointment with Mr. Harley, and fills the standish so full that the ink splashes on the writing paper. Yet he also appreciates the plays of Congreve, buys a linnet for Dingley, and has a wonderful art in "denying" his master to unwelcome visitors.

Another link with the past is an occasional reference to Moor Park. When he sees Temple's nephew and his wife pass in their coach, he takes no notice, and comments: "I am glad I have wholly shaken off that family." But another occasion is sadly disappointing to his vanity. He and Lady Giffard pass one another in "chariots" on the road between Windsor and London. But it happens just before Lord Oxford came along and took Swift into his coach: "so it happened that these people saw me, but not with Lord Treasurer."

However, no doubt Lady Giffard was well aware of the change in the fortunes of her brother's lowly secretary, just as Stella and Dingley knew what was keeping him in London. The Church business on which he had been sent over was soon settled, but the Tory politicians had discovered the extreme value to them of his pen and his brains. Six months after his arrival he wrote:

> I did not expect to find such friends as I have done . . . The assurances they give me, without scruple or provocation, are such as are usually believed in the world; they may come to nothing, but the first opportunity that offers and is neglected, I shall depend no more, but come away.

A year later the uncertainty is the same:

> I cannot leave this place in prudence or honour . . . I never wished so much as now that I had stayed in Ireland, but the die is cast and is now aspinning, and till it settle itself I cannot tell whether it be an ace or a six. I am confident . . . that you will justify me in all this.

This note sounds all through: "I long to be in Ireland, but the ministry beg me to stay," and he wonders if news of his importance has spread to Dublin: "Do they know anything in Ireland of my greatness among the Tories?" He dines constantly with Harley, who had confessed "that uttering his mind to me gave him ease." He is present at the inner conclaves of the chief ministers: "they let in none else," and are all "excessively obliging." He edits the weekly *examiner,* the Party paper and is "in furious haste" turning out pamphlets. Soon he feels his status is so firmly established that he can show his own mettle. When Harley is bad-tempered, Swift tells Stella he warned him "never to appear cold to me, for I would not be treated like a schoolboy, and that I had felt too much of that in my life already (meaning Sir William Temple)." When the Secretary of State tempts him to dinner by showing him the bill of fare, "Poh, said I, I value not your bill of fare, give me your bill of company."

No doubt Swift was arrogant about his phenomenal rise and made enemies, yet he combined it with a generous spirit and a hatred of the extravagance of party feuds. He was afraid his friendship with Addison "will go off by this damned business of party"; he helped both Steele and Congreve to keep the government jobs given them by the Whigs; and he found time apart from his politics to help struggling writers, to pray with sick friends, and to befriend poor widows and dull Irish acquaintances. But as he says: "I can serve everybody but myself." The tone of his comments, as well as the pace of his activities, becomes more agitated as time slips by. The ministry was falling apart. Harley and St. John had never worked well together and their mutual distrust steadily deepened. Swift was forever trying to play the part of honest go-between and patch things up:

> I have ventured all my credit with these great ministers to clear some misunderstandings. . . . If there be no breach, I ought to have the merit of it. 'Tis a plaguy ticklish piece of work and a man hazards losing both sides.

The great aim of the Tories was to make peace with France, and Swift bent all his literary genius to that cause in his pamphlet *The Conduct of the Allies,* published (anonymously of course) in November 1711. It soon had "a most prodigious run" and sold eleven thousand copies.

> The Tory lords and commons in Parliament argue all from it: and all agree that never anything of that kind was of so great consequence, or made so many converts.

But Swift is frantic at the dilatoriness of the government. Oxford (Harley), he says, is "the greatest procrastinator in the world," and when St. John postpones a conference with him, he bursts out:

> This is the fault of all the present ministers, teazing me to death for my assistance, laying the whole weight of their affairs upon it, yet slipping opportunities.

As the violence of the Whig opposition grew, and the negotiations with France dragged on, and the Tory influence weakened, it was only too clear that Swift's hopes for advancement and reward were not to be fulfilled. His enemies at the Court were powerful, and though it is very unlikely that poor stupid Queen Anne was capable of reading *A Tale of a Tub,* or making any judgment on its ironies, she was undoubtedly informed that Swift's religious views were suspect, and that he was more politician than priest. All Church appointments had to be approved by the Queen. As for his political friends, as long as he was of use to them, they had no incentive to recommend him elsewhere. He had told Stella that at the first opportunity offered that was neglected by his patrons, he would leave at once. But within six months the Bishoprics of Hereford, of Gloucester, of Dromore, of St. David's, and of Derry fell vacant, and the Deaneries of Carlisle, Ely, Lichfield, and Wells. On April 13, 1713, when his friend Erasmus Lewis breaks it to him that the latest appointments have been made and that he has got nothing, he reports to Stella:

> This is what I always foresaw. . . . I bid Mr. Lewis tell Lord Treasurer that I took nothing ill of him, but his not giving me timely notice, as he promised to do, if he found the Queen would do nothing for me.

There was hope that he might be made Prebend of Windsor, but again the Queen refused. The final plan was that the Dean of St. Patrick's should be promoted to Bishop of Dromore, and that the vacant deanery, which was in the gift of the Duke of Ormond, and not of the Queen, should go to Swift.

"I confess I thought the ministry would not let me go," he writes, and we can guess how much must have been behind that pathetic admission. Swift was to agree with Dorothy Osborne's mother: "it is impossible to believe people worse than they are." He was a beaten man. "Rot 'em for ungrateful dogs," he spits out in a mood of fury; "Burn all politics!"

> I am condemned to live again in Ireland, and all the Court and Ministry did for me was to let me choose my situation in a country where I am banished.

This last comment, however, was not written to his "dearest dear MD"—who loved living in Ireland. It was written to Hester Van Homrigh, the young woman who was present in London all the while Stella was absent in Dublin, and of whom we hear so remarkably little in the *Journal*. Her father was a Dutch merchant who had settled in Dublin and rose to be Lord Mayor of the city. On his death his widow moved with her children to London, and it was during that journey that Swift had first made their acquaintance. Soon after he arrived in

1710 he reports dining frequently at "Mrs. Van's," and a daughter's birthday is mentioned. Evidently these reports provoked some catty remark from Stella, for he answers: "You say they are of no consequence: why, they keep as good female company as I do male." Constant dinners and suppers continued, and when he is in Chelsea he keeps his gown and periwig at Mrs. Van's and changes on his way to Court or conference. Eighteen months later we hear: "Her eldest daughter is come of age, and going to Ireland to look after her fortune, and get it in her own hands." One suspects that this falsehood was to make Stella believe that he would not be seeing Miss Van Homrigh any more. But Hester did not go to Ireland, and the dangerous situation described later by Swift in the poem *Cadenus and Vanessa* was evidently already established. In that Cadenus sets out to be Vanessa's tutor, and to teach her "judgment, knowledge, wit and taste." In the poem, however, Vanessa declares:

> Your lessons found the weakest part,
> Aim'd at the head, but reach'd the heart.

Cadenus is flattered, but offers only warm friendship:

> A constant rational delight
> On virtue's basis fixed to last,
> When love's allurements long are past.

Vanessa won't accept this and decides to reverse their roles of teacher and pupil. The poem ends:

> But what success Vanessa met
> Is to the world a secret yet,
> Whether the nymph, to please her swain,
> Talks in a high romantic strain;
> Or whether he at last descends
> To like with less seraphic ends . . .
> Must never to mankind be told,
> Nor shall the concious Muse unfold.

We must go to the conscious letter-writers for any information about the "less seraphic ends," with the knowledge again of how imperfect it is, and of the lack of substantial evidence. The story runs—and this does have factual support—that on her deathbed in 1723, Vanessa gave instructions for the publication of Swift's letters to her, and copies of many of her own to him; that her executors, a young law clerk, Robert Marshall, and Dr. George Berkeley of Trinity College, Dublin (afterwards Bishop Berkeley, the philosopher), started arrangements for this, when Swift's friend Dr. Thomas Sheridan, and the Archbishop of Dublin brought such strong pressure against it that the plan was canceled. Dr. Berkeley later declared that he had read the letters and that there was nothing in them "which would either do honour to *her* character, or bring the least reflection on Cadenus." He said the letters had been destroyed.

In 1767, however, twenty-two years after Swift's death, some of them appeared as an appendix to an edition of Swift's letters, published in Dublin, with a note that the originals were in the hands of Robert Marshall, who had meanwhile become a Judge. No one knows what happened to them after that, until the originals turned up at a sale at Sotheby's in London in 1919. They are now in the British Museum.

The letters were carefully numbered by Vanessa, evidently as a help to her executors, and since many are missing, presumably Marshall removed them and destroyed them. The first was written in December 1711, fifteen months after his arrival in London and says: "Adieu, till we meet over a pot of coffee in the sluttery, which I have so often found to be the most agreeable chamber in the world." He encloses a letter to a mutual friend, which Vanessa is obviously intended to read; it praises her warmly, but hints that she is indiscreet: that she has a trick of sending her sister out of the room so that she can be alone with him, taking advantage of the fact that he is her tutor and so much older. He was in fact forty-four and Vanessa was twenty-two, and Swift was playing with fire, for Vanessa was no sweet compliant Stella, willing to keep the rules according to his prescription.

During the following spring and summer he wrote the *Journal* less frequently; giving health and work as reasons. All the old affection is still there, but less gay banter. But when he was at Windsor during that time, he and Vanessa were corresponding. He reiterated his longing to drink coffee in the sluttery and announced he was making plans to come to London and take a cheap lodging, "and dine with you thrice a week and will tell you a thousand secrets provided you will have no quarrel with me." It seems likely that *Cadenus and Vanessa* was written at this time.

By April 1712 Swift's fate was decided and in May, when he set out to be installed as Dean of St. Patrick's, he evidently intended a final break in the relationship with Vanessa. He wrote a short farewell note, thanking her for all her "kindness and generosity," and ends: "May God preserve you and make you happy . . . and so adieu, brat." His public reception was not friendly. On the day of the installation enemies nailed some scurrilous verses to the doors of the Cathedral:

> Today, this Temple gets a Dean,
> Of parts and fame uncommon;
> Used both to pray and to profane,
> To serve both God and Mammon . . .
> This place he got by wit and rhyme,
> And many ways most odd;
> And might a Bishop be in time,
> Did he believe in God.

Two weeks after the ceremony, he moved to his vicarage at Laracor, whose living he had retained. There he received four letters from Vanessa. She owns she is breaking a promise, but "I beg you won't be angry with me for doing what is not in my power to avoid." Swift's reply was curt: "I told you when I left England that I would endeavour to forget everything there, and would write as seldom as I could . . . If they [the ministry] have no further service for me, I will never see England again."

Unfortunately "they" summoned him back in a couple of months, and his hopes were raised that he might get some civil appointment; perhaps a diplomatic assignment abroad. He applied too for the post of Historiographer Royal, and tried at least to be paid a thousand pounds for the many expenses he had incurred during his service to the government. He failed again in all these ambitions. But in his relations with Vanessa this must have been the period of the "200 chapters of madness" he mentioned in a later letter. Mrs. Van Homrigh died that winter and Vanessa and her younger sister were independent. Queen Anne was dying and the split between Oxford and Bolingbroke became irreconcilable. The government fell, the Queen died, and Swift, from the house of a clergyman friend in the country, wrote to upbraid Vanessa for her indiscretion in paying him a surprise visit there. She had evidently told him of her intention to live with her sister on their Irish estate outside Dublin. Swift's letter is full of warnings and fears about it, all motivated, he says, by "perfect esteem and friendship." But he tries to be firm:

> If you are in Ireland when I am there I shall see you very seldom. It is not a place for any freedom; but where everything is known in a week, and magnified a hundred degrees.

Sybil de Brocuy, the author of the latest book on Vanessa, believes that not only were she and Swift lovers during this period, but that Vanessa had a child by him. We may not believe this, but it is impossible not to believe that Swift compromised himself deeply, and that his reputation was in her hands for the remaining nine years of her life. Even the existing letters are very damaging and probably the missing ones were more so. This would account for the fact that he was evidently not in a position to repudiate her entirely, in spite of frequent efforts to repel her with coldness and neglect. At the same time the tone of some of the later letters suggests that he was still bound to her by a sexual attraction, as well as by memories of the past—though of course he may simply have been flattering her to keep her quiet. Still, the constant references to the drinking of coffee and to some ritual "questions" which he must answer, certainly suggest some particular significance in their past relationship.

Anyhow, from November 1714 until April 1723 Swift was in the unenviable and dangerous position of having close open intimacy with one beloved young woman and secret, clandestine meetings and correspondence with another young woman, who had his good name in her hands; both living within a few miles of one another and of his Deanery. One of the stories, which we may or may not believe, was told in his later memoirs by Dr. Patrick Delaney, Fellow of Trinity College, and warm friend of Swift. He wrote that in 1716 he went to call on Dr. King, Archbishop of Dublin. He met Swift coming out, who rushed past him, his face distorted with emotion. Delaney found the Archbishop also in tears. "What is the matter with the Dean?" Delaney asked, and the Archbishop replied: "You have just seen the most unhappy man on earth, but on the subject of his wretchedness you must never ask a question." It seems clear that Swift and Vanessa met often in lodgings she took in Dublin, though he seldom went to Celbridge, her country house ten miles away. Her letters become those of a woman obsessed by a passion which absorbs her whole life. On her first arrival she pleads for practical help with her business affairs: "Pray, what can be wrong in seeing and advising an unhappy young woman?" We don't have Swift's answer but it caused her to reply: "I am sure I could have borne the rack much better than those killing, killing words of yours." Swift answered that: "Believe me it goes to my soul not to see you oftener . . . pray think it not a want of friendship and tenderness which I will always continue to the utmost." Another, undated, letter from Vanessa is a threat:

> Once more I advise you, if you have any regard for your own quiet, to alter your behaviour quickly, for I do assure you I have too much spirit to sit down contented with this treatment.

There seem to be no letters between 1715 and 1719, but the situation evidently remained explosive. Another undated one from Swift tells her that someone has repeated gossip to him that he and she are in love and that "little Master and I visited you—and twenty particulars." This is the chief piece of evidence that there was a child in the background. It is certainly a cryptic remark, but not supported by anything else in the surviving letters. Swift uses it to urge more discretion in her writing: "A stroke—signifies everything that may be said to Cad. at beginning or conclusion." In spite of his own warning, however, two extraordinary letters from Swift follow: one in French, full of extravagant praises of her person and personality, with a liberal supply of "strokes" at beginning and end; and a later one, suggesting that he should write a continuation of *Cadenus and Vanessa,* creating all the episodes of importance in their story since:

> . . . the adventures of the lost key . . . of the joyful return; 200 chapters of madness; the chapter of long walks; the Berkshire surprise; 50 chapters of little times . . . the chapter of hide and seek; the chapter of who made it so . . .

Yet a few months later, alone with her dying sister, Vanessa writes of his "prodigious neglect." She hasn't seen him for ten weeks, and she pours out her heart:

> It is not in the power of time or accident to lessen the inexpressible passion I have for you. Nor is the love I bear you only seated in my soul; for there is not a single atom in my frame that is not blended with it . . . Show some tenderness for me, or I shall lose my senses . . . You are present everywhere: your dear image is always before my eyes.

Her sister's death in March 1721 left Vanessa alone. A letter from Swift in July urges her to see her friends, take exercise, and finally: "Settle your affairs and quit this scoundrel island."

Nevertheless he adds in French: "But be assured no one in the world has been loved, honoured, esteemed, adored by your friend, but you." His remaining letters all urge exercise, reading, company, and acceptance of the human condition: "The best maxim I know in this life is, to drink your coffee when you can, and when you cannot, to be easy without it." This letter too, however, evokes, in French, memories of long mornings and evenings together in the past, each of which had its "agréments particuliers."

That was in the late summer of 1722, and what of Stella all this while? Swift saw her very frequently, he wrote verses to her for every birthday, praising her "breeding, humour, wit and sense," her "manly soul," her kindness, her loyalty, and his own unshakeable devotion to her. In only one set of verses, in 1720, does he deplore a "weaker side," when on one occasion "truth, judgment, wit give place to spite,/Regardless both of wrong and right." We can guess the subject of Stella's anger, for it was inconceivable that in Dublin, "where everything is known in a week," she did not know something at least of what was going on.

The story of a secret marriage between Swift and Stella started very early. It was spoken of as a fact in 1723, as we shall see later. Stella was also alleged to have confessed it on her deathbed to Dr. Sheridan. Yet she describes herelf in her will, drawn shortly before her death, as "spinster"—a description not required by law—and Rebecca Dingley and Swift's housekeeper both ridiculed the rumor. What possible benefit to her there would have been in a marriage which was to remain concealed and unconsummated, and made absolutely no difference to their way of life, is indeed difficult to see. It would do nothing to stop the gossip.

The reason for the final rupture between Swift and Vanessa again rests on nothing but gossip. No letters survive written in the last ten months of Vanessa's life. One story goes that

Vanessa wrote to Stella asking if she were married to Swift, that he rode out to Celbridge, flung the letter on the table and stalked out. Another version is that Stella confirmed the marriage and that Swift brought this letter. Sybil de Brocuy thinks Vanessa, knowing she was dying, wrote, telling her side of the story, and asking Stella to look after the child; that this was the first Stella had heard of the child and that Swift was furious with Vanessa for betraying the secret. We can never know. That there was *some* spectacular final rupture is certain, which caused Vanessa to alter her will, give all her fortune to strangers, and to try and arrange for the immediate publication of the letters. Swift obviously expected a scandal to break. The day after her death, he left the Deanery, without even giving an address to his vicar in the Cathedral. Nothing was heard from him for two months, when he wrote from the south of Ireland saying he would not return for some weeks. Stella and Dingley went to a friend's house in the country and stayed for six months. Dublin must have been buzzing with rumors, and a letter turned up about fifty years ago in the library of Christ's Church, Oxford, which outlines them. It was written on July 27th by the Bishop of Meath to the Archbishop of Canterbury:

> I think it not improper for me to acquaint your Grace with a passage lately happened here, wherein Jonathan Swift is said to be pretty much concerned. A young woman, Mrs. Van Omrig (a pretended vain wit) and the Dean had great friendships, many letters and papers passed betwixt them; they give out there was a marriage promise between them, but this I cannot affirm. However it be, she designed to give him all her fortune. . . . In April last she discovered the Dean was married to Mrs. Johnson (a natural daughter of Sir Wm. Temple, a very good woman) upon which she expressed great indignation, making a new will and leaving all to Dr. Berkeley and to one Mr. Marshall, who was charged by her (on her deathbed) to print all the letters and papers. . . . The Archbishop of Dublin and the whole Irish posse have (I fear) prevailed with Mr. Marshall not to print the papers etc. as she desired . . .

Swift did indeed miraculously escape a public scandal. A copy of *Cadenus and Vanessa* leaked out, but that was all. The Archbishop no doubt muzzled the clergy; all Swift's men friends held their tongues; Mr. Marshall was discreet and agreed to suppress publication and probably destroyed the most compromising letters; Dr. Berkeley was more than discreet, for he lied about their contents. It all died down. The following year Swift was a popular hero in Ireland as the author of the *Drapier's Letters*. . .

Stella lived for another five years, but how frightened Swift was of any further scandal can be seen in a letter he wrote to his vicar, John Worrall, when he was in London and feared Stella might die during his absence. He is in an agony of anxiety and grief:

> There is not a greater folly than too great and intimate a friendship, which must always leave the survivor miserable. . . . Believe me violent friendship is much more lasting and as much engaging as violent love.

Yet in the midst of this anguish, he inserts a passage in Latin to say that on no account must Stella die in the Deanery, since it would not be decent and his enemies would interpret it maliciously. To another friend he reports that he is sick and does not care if he recovers, since he must face the loss of "that person for whose sake only life is worth preserving." His only reason for wanting to return to the hated land of Ireland is to see her once more. But he could not face being present at her death: "I should be a trouble to her and a torment to myself . . . I could not behave myself tolerably."

Nor could he face the funeral, and moved into another room so that he could not see the lights in the Cathedral. Then he sat down, alone, to put upon paper something of Stella's "life and character." He tried to communicate some idea of her beauty, her intelligence, her gentleness, her courage, her generosity, her absolute integrity, and her vivacious charm. But somehow the words communicate little and Stella remains as elusive as ever. We cannot doubt that he speaks truth when he describes her as "the most disinterested mortal I ever knew or heard of," and that she was indeed "the truest, most virtuous and valuable friend that I, or perhaps any other person, was ever blessed with." No woman could have a more loving and heartfelt eulogy, and she must have been fully aware, during her lifetime, of all she meant to him. But how much did she really know about Vanessa? And what were Swift's feelings during all those years when he had these anomalous relations with these two women? Poor passion-ravaged Vanessa is the only one of the trio whose emotions are no enigma, though the facts about her actions remain obscure.

Swift was to live another seventeen years after Stella's death —until he was seventy-seven. Alas for our curiosity that he kept so faithfully the resolutions about old age that he had made on Sir William Temple's death: "Not to talk of myself . . . Not to boast of my former beauty, or strength, or favour with the ladies etc." Swift did not talk: he took all his secrets with him to the grave.

# Lady Mary Wortley Montagu

1689-1762

SHE HAD PARTS, and had seen much," said Horace Walpole, by way of epitaph on Lady Mary Wortley Montagu; a woman he had always disliked and maligned, and whom he referred to elsewhere as "that old, foul, tawdry, painted, plastered personage." She was a woman, nevertheless, whom he never missed meeting, and about whose personality he kept an inextinguishable curiosity to the end. And it is no wonder that the most inquisitive mind of the eighteenth century interested itself in that figure, for it is surely that of the most remarkable and original—if not the most estimable—woman of the age.

It was an age which did not encourage Englishwomen to be remarkable or original. As Lady Mary herself commented, as a result of her wide travels: "To say truth, there is no part of the world where our sex is treated with so much contempt as in England." Women were expected to accept the doctrine which Lady Mary, as a girl, states to the Bishop of Salisbury, as she apologizes for aspiring to translate Epictetus:

> I do not doubt God and Nature have thrown us into an inferior rank. We are a lower part of the creation, and we owe obedience and submission to the superior sex.

No wonder she bitterly regretted being born a woman, and in her old age, summed up its disabilities so shrewdly as she congratulates her daughter on the birth of a son:

> I am never in pain for any of that sex. If they have any merit, there are so many roads for them to meet good fortune they

> can no way fail of it but by not deserving it. We have but one way of establishing ours, and that surrounded by precipices, and perhaps, after all, better missed than found.

She, at any rate, did not achieve good fortune by the one way open to women of her time—the way of marriage. After about fifteen years of married life, she wrote in disillusion to her sister: "Don't you remember how miserable we were in the little parlour at Thoresby? We then thought marrying would put us at once into possession of all we wanted." Those were the days when the two eldest of the three motherless daughters of the Earl of Kingston were spending their childhood more or less bringing themselves up at their father's house in Nottinghamshire. The eldest, Lady Mary Pierrepoint, had unusual tastes. Reading was a passion with her; she taught herself Latin, Greek, French, and Italian, and spent most of her time in the library, devouring everything from contemporary sentimental romances to the classical poets. Thirty miles away, at Wharncliffe Lodge, lived the Hon. Sidney Montagu, who had taken the name of Wortley on inheriting his wife's money. His daughter, Anne Wortley, was one of Lady Mary's friends and his son Edward was to be her husband. (He is usually called Mr. Wortley, but Lady Mary seems to have preferred the double version.)

It is not difficult to understand the original attraction between the two young people, but that the relationship reached marriage, or that either of them really expected it to prove a happy marriage, is astonishing to any reader of their courtship correspondence. Edward Wortley was a handsome, humorless young man, who belonged in a literary "set." He had traveled abroad with Addison, and Steele had dedicated the second volume of *The Tatler* to him. It was quite natural that at the age of thirty-one, he should fall in love with a girl of twenty, who could appeal not only by her beauty, but also by a mind interested in all his own literary pursuits, and who could flatter him by grossly overrating his own very moderate talents. It was very natural that a girl of twenty, to whom reading was the most important thing in life, should fall in love with this older man, on terms of friendship with some of the leading literary lights of the day, who admired her serious interests and at the same time fell a victim to her feminine charms.

But the sequel was not natural. Mr. Wortley becomes more and more priggish and self-complacent; he is maddeningly cautious about taking any decisive step and maddeningly suspicious of her worthiness to be his wife. As she very justly remarks, he is always full of "scruples, suspicions, cross-questions and ill-nature." In general she is patient: "I can bear being told I am in the wrong, but tell it me gently," she pleads; but she also has spirit, and in November 1710, she bursts out:

> I begin to be tired of my humility: I have carried my complacence to you further than I ought. You make new scruples . . . and your distrusts, being all of your own making, are more immovable than if there were some real grounds for them. . . . You say you are not determined: let me determine for you and save you the trouble. . . . Adieu for ever.

This did produce a formal application to her father, now Marquess of Dorchester, for her hand, but the men could not agree on the terms of the settlement. The match was broken off and Lady Mary forbidden to see her lover. Presumably it was the ban placed on their relationship which made it so valuable to her, for otherwise it is almost impossible to understand how she could put up with his criticisms of her in the next year. He accuses her of coldness, while he himself retreats if she shows the slightest warmth; he makes her behave indiscreetly by meeting him in secret, and then blames her for indiscretion; if she makes light of his suspicions it proves she does not care for him, while if she flares into indignation he replies: "Your resenting what I said, is an argument of it being pretty near the truth." But in spite of each of them declaring over and over how unsuited they are, neither seems capable of making a final breach. In the summer of 1712, however, when she is within a few weeks of being married off to the son of an Irish peer approved by her father, Mr. Wortley agrees to an elopement. He is not enthusiastic, but says he will provide the coach, and adds: "If we should once get into the coach, let us not say one word till we come before the parson, lest we engage in fresh disputes." However she is evidently convinced by his willingness to take her "with only a nightgown and a petticoat" that his feeling is sincere, and at the very end he lowers his defenses: "I can no longer forbear laying my heart quite open and telling you the joy I am in for being so near the greatest happiness I am capable of enjoying."

Once married, however, it all starts again. They had argued before about living in town or country and she had said: "Very few people who have settled entirely in the country, but have grown at length weary of one another." Soon it is clear what his plan is. She is to spend all her time in the country, while he makes his headquarters in London. So for more than two years we follow Lady Mary, either quartered on her husband's relations or puting up with uncomfortable furnished houses, while he pays occasional visits. It is clear that in the unfortunate way of women, she is more in love with her husband since marriage, while his passion has cooled on possession. Even the birth of their son does not rouse any interest and she tries in vain to charm him out of his coldness:

> My dear Life, write to me, take care of your health and let me see you as soon as you can. Your little boy delivered me your letter. The nurse thought it would be an acceptable present and put it into his hands. You will laugh at this circumstance, which you will think very ridiculous, but it pleased me mightily.

Neither wifely solicitude nor maternal tenderness seemed to touch Mr. Wortley, and at last Lady Mary's patience was exhausted, she "suffered her inclination to get the better of her reason," and sat down to some plainspeaking:

> I know very well that nobody was ever teased into a liking . . . but I cannot forbear any longer telling you I think you use me very unkindly. . . . You seem perfectly pleased with our separation and indifferent how long it continues. . . . A little kindness will cost you nothing.

She roundly attacks his silence, the "nothingness" of his letters, his lack of affection for his child, and his callous unconcern about her own loneliness and ill-health.

The letter may have had some effect, but Mr. Wortley also won a lucrative appointment to the Treasury, and in January 1715, Lady Mary moved to a house in London, and at once took her place as one of the handsomest and wittiest women there. A year later the opportunity came for what was much dearer to her than fashionable London life: foreign travel. Mr. Wortley was appointed ambassador at Constantinople, and those letters of hers were written which were the only memorable result of his otherwise colorless embassy. These letters were probably composed for publication from her diaries and from copies of some of the originals, but though she skillfully mingles serious and comedy material in them, they have none of the spontaneous warmth of those about her later travels. Yet they are full of vitality and interest in all she sees and hears and does. She wrote later of a Turkish acquaintance: "She is very curious after the manners of other countries, and has not the partiality for her own so common in little minds." The words apply equally well to herself. She is entirely without insularity and prejudice and possesses an insatiable appetite for new experiences. They traveled, with an enormous retinue, overland to Constantinople, "a journey not undertaken by any Christian for some hundred years," she declares. They visit the various European courts, and in each she finds something which her own country might well imitate. She would have the London stage as civilized as that of Paris; the London streets as clean and free from beggars as those of The Hague; and she comments on the "obstinacy" of her own people who prefer "to shake with cold six months of the year" instead of borrowing the idea of the convenient and ornamental German stoves.

When she arrives in Turkey, she reports every aspect of its culture and mores: history, religion, society, housing, husbandry, gardens, music, dancing, clothes. She copies oriental love-poems, makes the acquaintance of scholarly Turks and collects Greek coins. She learns of the custom of inoculation for smallpox and has her own little boy immunized. She is lyrical about the charm of the Turkish women, and the beauty of a scene in a marble "bagnio," though to join the ladies in the bath is one of the experiences she refuses:

> I excused myself with some difficulty. They being all so earnest in persuading me, I was at last forced to open my skirt and show them my stays; which satisfied them . . . for I saw they believed I was so locked up in that machine, that it was not in my power to open it; which contrivance they attributed to my husband.

She tells her women correspondents of the Turkish custom of shaping eyebrows and of the secrets of eye-shadow, "but 'tis too visible by day"; also the fashion of dyeing the nails a rose color. She was not fortunate, however, over an experiment with the miraculous "Balm of Mecca":

> I had a present of a small quantity of the best sort, and with great joy applied it to my face, expecting some wonderful effect to my advantage. The next morning the change indeed was wonderful; my face had swelled to a very extraordinary size, and all over as red as my Lady B's. It remained in this lamentable state three days, during which time you may be sure I passed my time very ill . . . and to add to my mortification Mr. Wortley reproached my indiscretion without ceasing.

Lady Mary's new experiences, however, successful or otherwise, were cut short the following year. Mr. Wortley was recalled from his Embassy in less than six months after his arrival, and he and his wife, the little boy of five, and the baby girl born in Constantinople, returned to England. Mr. Wortley remained a member of Parliament all his life, but never held any further office. They rented a town house in Covent Garden and a country house at Twickenham, and Lady Mary was soon in the thick of court society and the literary wits. She was now thirty, and had lost her youthful illusions and freshness of emotion, without developing yet any of the wisdom and warmth of heart which made her lovable in old age. It seems indeed as if all Mr. Wortley's early doubts about her discretion and dignity were well-founded, and though the witty malice of her gossip to her sister Lady Mar (exiled in Paris with her Jacobite husband) makes very entertaining reading, her ruthlessness with the reputations of others makes it difficult to sympathize much with the probably equally slanderous attacks brought against herself. She was one of the many who thought to enrich themselves in the boom of the South Sea Company. She not only bought stock in it herself, but also persuaded a young Frenchman, Nicolas-François Rémond, with whom she had been having a flirtatious correspondence, to entrust his money to her. When the boom turned into the Bubble six months later, and the investments were lost, he accused her of trickery, and threatened to tell her husband and send him her letters.

Again and again she implores Lady Mar to explain her innocence to Rémond and get him to call off his persecution. Finally, it seems as if she either managed to repay him his original investment or confessed her foolishness to her husband and left matters in his hands. A few years later, however, she was involved in a far more important quarrel, with an old friend who turned into her bitterest enemy. Before her visit to Turkey, Pope had been one of her chief admirers. During her absence he had written extravagantly that she had spoiled him for the company of men, women, and books, and that if he were to write to her as often as he thought of her, it would be every day of her life. In the early days after her return the intimacy continued. A malicious Twickenham neighbor wrote:

"She and Pope keep so close yonder that they are a talk to the whole town. . . . They say a great many things of her using Mr. Wortley like a dog." Pope commissioned the aging Sir Godfrey Kneller to paint a portrait of her: the face, with its shapely mouth and nose and large dark eyes, and the beautiful neck above the very low-cut bodice, are very seductive.

No one knows what caused the breach. Pope declared he suspected her of lampooning him in a satirical sketch. She denied this and it was suggested later, though not by her, that he had made a passionate declaration of love and that she had laughed at him. Anyhow whether the insult was real or imaginary it roused all the venomous malice of "the wicked wasp of Twickenham." For seven years he introduces the character of "Sappho" into his satires in order to besmirch her as a cheat, a slut, a miser and a whore. Lady Mary foolishly, but perhaps very naturally, asked friends to protest the worst of these attacks. But Pope's position was of course unassailable. He had never mentioned her by name, and as Lord Peterborough, one of her emissaries, reported back to her: "He said to me, what I had already taken the liberty of saying to you, that he wondered how the town could apply the lines to any but some noted common woman: and that he would yet be more surprized if *you* should take them to yourself."

Lady Mary was certainly more or less notorious for being careless in dress and stingy in money matters, and the Rémond affair could be made to look like swindling, but no one except Pope ever mentions sexual promiscuity. Nor has it ever been proved that she was the author of any anonymous attacks on Pope. Nevertheless she was a controversial figure. She wrote verse satires herself, and her house was a center for young musicians and writers. She liked to play the patroness and critic to aspiring artists; and when her cousin, Henry Fielding, came to London in 1727, at the age of twenty, she urged the managers of Drury Lane Theater to take his first comedy. She was admired by Voltaire, and was a friend of

Mary Astell, an early supporter of women's rights. Lady Mary wrote anonymous articles for her in favor of easier divorce and the abolition of marriage dowries. She waged a courageous campaign against doctors and clergy in support of inoculation for smallpox. It was no fault of hers that her private family affairs became matters of public gossip. Her sister Lady Mar suffered a mental breakdown in 1728, and as a good deal of money was involved, a legal struggle with her husband's relatives, and even a practical kidnaping had to be dealt with before the Court finally put her in the custody of Lady Mary. Then from 1726 until the end of their lives she and her husband were plagued by the problem of their no-good son. That baby who had delighted her so much grew up to be a thorough rogue. At the age of thirteen he ran away from Westminster School and was found in Oxford: "being in his own opinion thoroughly qualified for a university"; the next year he ran away to sea, and six months later was brought home from Gibraltar. After several years of travel with a tutor, he married a woman "of very low degree," much older than himself, whom he promptly deserted, and then went "from one species of folly to another." He sponged continually on his parents; forged his mother's signature to a check in Venice; was involved in a robbery in Paris and imprisoned; made several bigamous marriages and left several illegitimate children.

Lady Mary was soon completely disillusioned about any reform in young Edward. She hoped, however, that her daughter Mary would make a brilliant marriage. Here too, she was disappointed. The girl refused several promising suitors and instead, when she was eighteen, fell in love with the young Scottish Earl of Bute, handsome and well-born, but quite poor. Both Mr. Wortley and Lady Mary did their best to block the marriage, but the young people persisted. The wedding was in 1736 and they went to live in Scotland.

In that year, too, Lady Mar's daughter was old enough to take over the custody of her mother, which released Lady

Mary from that responsibility. She was free, in her late forties, to enter into a tragi-comic relationship which was to change the whole course of her life. It has long been debated what caused her to leave England in 1739 and to spend almost the whole of the rest of her life abroad. It was common gossip that her marriage was by this time quite loveless. Mr. Wortley devoted himself entirely to his parliamentary duties and his business interests, which were very large. He had a general reputation for dullness, for coldness, and for avarice. Lady Mary was always discretion itself about her relations with her husband. She is cynical enough about marriage in general, but she never discusses Mr. Wortley with any of her correspondents and she always loyally praises him to her children. She tells her daughter later: "I know him to be more capable of a generous action than any man I ever knew." Yet it is clear that they never had any of that "satisfaction at home," which as she says: "is what sweetens all the accidents of life and can be made up by no other advantages where it is wanting." We can only guess how her brilliance compared with his own nonentity, her delight in the limelight, her indiscretions and imprudencies and amateur dabblings in finance, must have bred resentments in him and offended his sense of conventional propriety, even if they resulted in no open scandal. It was generally thought, therefore, that the suggestion of a separation had probably come from him.

But as a result of the researches of Lady Mary's latest biographer, Robert Halsband, we now know the facts behind her exile and the whole drama of her relations with Francesco Algarotti. Algarotti was a young Italian commoner, who had made a name for himself in both science and letters in his own country and in France. He arrived in London in the spring of 1736, with an introduction from Voltaire to Lord Hervey, and recommendations to members of the Royal Society, into which he was at once received. Lord Hervey, favorite at Court, and also bitter enemy of Pope, was a great friend of Lady Mary: her remark on him is well known—that there were three sexes, men, women, and Herveys. He introduced her to Algarotti and she recalls later that in less than fifteen days he had won her heart. She had indeed become completely infatuated with this young stranger of half her age, who moreover was as fond of relations with his own sex as of those with women. She soon discovered that Lord Hervey too was equally captivated by Algarotti's charms, and both of them competed for his attentions. When he made known his intention of returning to Italy in the summer, Lady Mary wrote that she saw all the folly of her feelings without the possibility of correcting them, and when he had left she pursued him with letters expressing her passionate devotion. It is indeed extraordinary to read these love letters in the light of her earlier forms of expression. The proud girl, the poised, sophisticated traveler, the society scandal-mongerer, the satiric versifier and pamphleteer are all forgotten as this middle-aged woman pours out all her repressed tenderness and emotional warmth. Lord Hervey too bombarded Algarotti with letters urging his return. He was equally unmoved, however by either of his mature adorers, and wrote very seldom. Lady Mary twice makes the suggestion that if he cannot return to England, she will join him in Italy: "This sounds extraordinary, and yet it is not so when you consider the impression you have made on a heart that is capable of receiving no other."

Finally in the autumn of 1738, after a summer spent with a new young friend of his own sex, Algarotti wrote that he could not afford to come to England unless Lady Mary could provide the funds: which, needless to say, she did. He arrived in March 1739 and stayed for a while with Lord Hervey. Finding, however, that Hervey was no longer as influential as he had been at Court and in politics, he moved to richer patrons, among them Lord Burlington, who had a magnificent house at Chiswick, near Twickenham. When he and Lady Mary met, according to her account, he promised to retire with her to Venice and bring her undreamt-of happiness. She put it about that she had a longing to see Italy again, and planned a trip abroad for her health. We have no reason to believe that anyone except Hervey knew the real stimulus behind her move, and he loyally kept her secret. Mr. Wortley put no obstacle in her way, but arranged a generous allowance for her travels and they continued to correspond amicably for the next twenty years without ever meeting again. She set out in July 1739, at the age of fifty, writing to Algarotti the day before she left "full of faith and hope" as she sets out for "another world."

> If I find what you have sworn to me, I find the Elysian fields, and happiness beyond imagination.

Future developments can be guessed. Algarotti made a short visit to the court of the Crown Prince of Prussia (later Frederick the Great). The Prince was immensely taken with him and though Algarotti returned to England, kept urging him to come back to Rheinsberg. Algarotti wrote occasionally to Lady Mary in Venice, shifting their meeting place from Venice to Paris, to Switzerland and finally to Holland, but she refused these invitations, though she continued to write in the same impassioned way. Then a letter from Lord Hervey told her that Prince Frederick had become King and had immediately summoned Algarotti to him. He was given the title of Count and sent on a secret diplomatic mission to Turin. Whether or not encouraged by him, Lady Mary arrived at Turin, and as may be imagined, the meeting was disastrous. In place of the "taste, delicacy and vivacity" she had found before, nothing is now revealed but "grossness and indifference." Her disenchantment was complete, and at last she saw her five-year infatuation for what it was, and scorns herself for it as much as she scorns him. She confessed her humiliation to Hervey, who wrote kindly about "this very disagreeable episode in your life," and advised her to bury it and find consolation elsewhere.

It is not surprising that this strange adventure remained a secret for so long, for in her letters to others and in descriptions of her by others, she remains quite unchanged. For some time she maintained the fiction that Mr. Wortley was to join her as soon as his parliamentary duties permitted, but meanwhile she established herself in the cosmopolitan world of Venice, and rattled off accounts of its customs, its scenery and its scandals to her friends. She went on to Florence, Rome, Naples, and Leghorn before the visit to Turin, and after that to Genoa, Geneva, and finally Avignon. Throughout she wrote long serious letters to her husband. Probably very well aware of how much she has been gossiped about in London, and how much Mr. Wortley disliked it, she is specially anxious to impress upon him how respectfully she is received wherever she goes. From Venice she writes: "I verily believe if one of the pyramids of Egypt had travelled, it could not have been more followed," and from Rome: "Though it may sound a little vain to say it, the young English travellers really paid a little court to me, as if I had been their queen." It is true that one of the "governors" of the young travelers, Joseph Spence, left a description of her as "one of the most extrordinary shining characters," but he adds that she is many-sided and can be "the most wise, most imprudent; loveliest, disagreeablest; best-natured, cruelest woman in the world." It is to be feared, as Mr. Wortley was probably already aware, that Lady Mary was not always very sensitive to what impression she was really making. "I was very well acquainted with Mr. Walpole in Florence," she tells her daughter, "and indeed he was particularly civil to me." Young Horace Walpole's own account is rather different.

> Did I tell you Lady Mary Wortley is here? She is laughed at by the whole town. Her dress, her avarice and her impudence, must amaze anyone that never heard her name. She wears a foul mob, that does not cover her greasy black locks . . . an old mazzarine blue wrapper, that gapes open and

> discovers a canvas petticoat. Her face swelled violently on one side . . . partly covered with white paint, which for cheapness she has bought so coarse, that you would not use it to wash a chimney.

One suspects that this is a second-hand report from some malicious caller who found her in *deshabille,* and even Walpole adds: "but she is very entertaining." It is probable, however, that Lady Mary was not earning quite all the admiration she would have Mr. Wortley believe.

She stayed four years in Avignon, finding it a place where "one can while away an idle life with great tranquility: which has long since been the utmost of my ambition." She seems to have been much respected there for her literary and social gifts, and we have good proofs of it from other sources than her own letters. After the failure of the Jacobite rebellion in 1745, however, Avignon became crowded with the exiled supporters of the Young Pretender. The war with France interfered too with correspondence from England and makes her feel as if she were "the inhabitant of another planet." The English were also fighting with the Austrians against Spain and France in northern Italy, where she wished to return.

All this led to another strange relationship in her life, where again she became the dupe of an unscrupulous and plausible young man, though with him she lost only her head and not her heart. Count Ugolino Palazzi, thirty-year-old heir of an old but impoverished Brescian family, called on Lady Mary with an introduction from a mutual friend in Venice. He was on his way home from the court of Saxony, where he had served the Prince as gentleman of the bedchamber. Hearing of Lady Mary's wish to reach northern Italy, and her fear of traveling alone, he offered to be her escort. The plan was that she should pretend to be a Venetian lady returning home. It was completely successful, and though they met some Spanish and Austrian troops and were delayed in the confusion, they reached Brescia in ten days. There the Count's mother welcomed Lady

Mary and insisted that she stay with her until she had found a house for herself. Lady Mary reports all these facts to her husband, but says nothing about any financial arrangements with the Count; indeed we should know nothing of them had she not written a detailed account of it all in a manuscript which has never been published, but which Robert Halsband found and studied. From this, it is clear that they did not leave Avignon until she had "loaned" the Count a considerable sum of money, and during the next ten years he seems to have tricked her by one shady scheme after another. His arrangements for having her house-furnishings and possessions transported from Avignon resulted in the mysterious loss of some valuable furniture and china and some jeweled snuffboxes; he sold her a tumbledown old "palace" and a neglected garden for far more than their value; and staged what she herself was convinced was a bogus robbery of her jewel-box during one of her absences from home.

Apart from all this, this retreat among the Italian lakes proved the perfect setting for Lady Mary's declining years, which were sweetened and softened by the unclouded intimacy with her daughter, Lady Bute, to whom most of her letters are addressed. They are the most delightful she ever wrote. However much she was swindled over her palace, she loved it, and specially the garden, about a mile away, on the banks of a river, and adjoined by a wood, where she built "bowers" to rest in. One, near the river-bank, served as a camp kitchen, where she could eat fish freshly caught and cooked, and watch the ships passing. She declares she is as fond of the garden as a young author of his first play, and she loves to talk about it: "gardening is certainly the next amusement to reading." She spends most of her time actively engaged there and in the dairy, or tending her poultry, bees, and silkworms, all of which prosper and give employment to the peasants. She teaches the country folk around to make French rolls, and

English butter and custards, mince pies, and plum pudding. She rides, walks, and fishes, and as her eyes permit only a few hours' reading, she spends the evenings with the local gentry, or teaching the old priests from the village how to play whist and piquet.

It was natural that her retirement in such a happy environment, and her harmonious relationship with her daughter, should bring Lady Mary a mellowness of outlook which she had never possessed before. She had little to trouble her. Every now and then some exploit of "that knavish fool," her scapegrace son, comes to her ears, or she has a mood of chilling boredom, but she has found a new peace:

> There is quiet after the abandoning of pursuits like the rest that follows a laborious day. . . . It was formerly a terrifying view to me that I should one day be an old woman. I now find that nature has provided pleasures for every state. Those only are unhappy who will not be contented with what she gives, but strive to break her laws by affecting a perpetuity of youth.

As for herself, as she finds ugliness and wrinkles "mortifying" she adopts the logical solace of not using a mirror, and declares in 1757 that she hasn't looked at her face for eleven years. She never has "the vapours," does not suffer from the delusion that the world was better in her youth, and at sixty-two can enjoy active exercise, has an excellent appetite and sound sleep, perfect hearing and a clear memory, and on finding a box of books has arrived from England when she comes in from a twenty-mile ride at ten o'clock at night, she opens it and sits up till dawn reading Fielding's *Joseph Andrews*.

Her philosophy in general is a ripe and vigorous rationalism. In the light of our new knowledge of her own sexual infatuation, we open our eyes somewhat at her comment on the mistaken marriage of a rich widow to a much younger man: "If she thought justly she would know that no man ever was in love with a woman of forty, since the Deluge"; and similar bits of moral superiority clash rather comically with her own notorious folly and failings. Yet she will then disarm us by a candid confession of how we all humbug ourselves: "all that experience can do is to mitigate, we can never extinguish our passions"; and urge the innocent gratification of the senses and to live to the full in the present: "it is all that is properly ours."

With admirable common sense she deplores what she regards as the enemies of enlightenment: "the quackery of churches"; the "palpable folly" of war—"fully as senseless as the boxing of schoolboys"; political hypocrisy; the credulous use of "universal medicines" and the foolishness of parents:

> We mothers should take example of the innocuous inhabitants of the air; when their young are fledged they are delighted to see them fly and peck for themselves. Forgive this freedom. I have no other receipt for maternal fondness, a distemper which has long afflicted.

She can even find comfort in her separation from her daughter, as they would be sure to disagree about the upbringing of the children, and "the affection of a grandmother has generally a tincture of dotage." There is little sign of dotage, though, in the advice she gives Lady Bute over and over again, to try and bring up the children free of prejudice and to encourage in them a love of reading: "There is no entertainment so cheap; nor any pleasure so lasting."

Lady Mary's criticism of books are the best-known part of her letters. Anyone who has ever studied eighteenth-century literature has read her appreciation of Fielding's vitality and her summing up of Richardson's *Pamela* as "the joy of chambermaids of all nations." But as she got older she cares for little but "the gay part of reading." She asks for a constant supply of sentimental romances and frivolous memoirs, and in a letter of 1757, when she is sixty-eight, she makes a famous defense of her pastime:

> Daughter, daughter! don't call names. . . . Trash, lumber, sad stuff are the titles you give to my favorite amuse-

> ment . . . we all have our playthings; happy are those who can be contented with those they can obtain. . . . Your youngest son is perhaps at this very moment riding on a poker with great delight, not at all regretting that it is not a gold one, and much less wishing it an Arabian horse. . . . I am reading an idle tale, not expecting wit or truth in it, and am very glad it is not metaphysics to puzzle my judgments, or history to mislead my opinion. . . . He fortifies his health by exercise; I calm my cares by oblivion. . . . If he improves his health and I forget my infirmities, we attain very desirable ends.

This letter was written from Venice, where Lady Mary had arrived the year before after having been practically held to ransom by Count Palazzi. Her health had begun to fail, she wanted to be among friends and in more certain correspondence with England. The Count, however, refused to make any arrangements for her journey unless she made over to him all the property she had bought from him, trying to blackmail her by a threat to ruin her reputation by declaring that their relations of the past ten years had been amorous! She finally reached Venice safely and threatened to prosecute the Count, but nothing came of it. An English acquaintance in Venice commented—to Algarotti of all people!—"She is more ashamed, I believe, for passing for a dupe in the eye of the public, than she is for passing for a woman of gallantry." Algarotti, after many years in Prussia, had retired to Bologna. He and Lady Mary exchanged cordial letters; he offered her the use of his villa in his absence; they exchanged and admired each other's writings; but they did not meet.

She found old friends and made new ones, for she was still full of vitality and cultural curiosity, of racy conversation and vigor of mind. When Mr. Wortley congratulates her on the continuation of her spirits in her letters, she replies: " 'Tis true, I try to maintain them by every art I can, being sensible of the terrible consequence of losing them." But a great deal of her taste for the simple life of her eleven-year exile evaporates when she has left her garden and her solitude and is back in the competitive social world. "I am afraid we are little better than straws upon the water; we flatter ourselves we swim, when the current carries us along." What she had thought was maturity and serenity had been only lack of opportunity to involve herself in controversial relationships. "I give myself admirable advice, but am incapable of taking it" she confesses ruefully, with the result that she is soon in the midst of a bitter quarrel with the British Resident, which must on no account reach Mr. Wortley's ears: "Do not tell your father these foolish squabbles . . . I am apprehensive he should imagine some misplaced raillery or vivacity of mine has drawn on me this ridiculous persecution."

In January 1761, however, Mr. Wortley died, and his disapproval, so much dreaded apparently even when she was seventy and he over eighty, troubled her no more. He left an immense fortune in money, land, and mines to Lady Bute, but only an annuity of a thousand pounds to his widow. She began to make plans for a return to England. Her health was now bad. With her usual ability to find a telling image she says caring for it has become "like mending old lace, when it is patched in one place, it breaks in another." Yet with her usual spirit she set out at the age of seventy-two, with some foreign servants, on the toilsome journey. She was held up for two months, by weather and sickness, at Rotterdam, and while there, lodged with the Reverend Benjamin Sowden, minister of the English Church. To him she consigned the manuscript of her Turkish Embassy letters, with the evident understanding that he should publish them after her death.

She arrived in London in January 1762. Lord Bute had steadily gained in political influence and court favor, and on the accession of George III in 1760 had been made a member of the Privy Council. His wife, now the mother of ten children, was a close friend of the Queen. She was definitely her father's daughter and doubtless shared the popular opinion that the arrival of Lady Mary might bring troubles. But Horace Walpole reported after she had been back a couple of months: "She is much more discreet than I expected, and meddles with nothing." Her reputation was still very much alive and her vitality still undimmed. Mrs. Montague, the bluestocking, declared she still had the vivacity of a girl and that "she neither thinks, speaks, acts or dresses like anybody else." Walpole, of course, emphasizes her avarice and slovenly surroundings and clothes, but finds her face almost unchanged, though her conversational brilliance dimmed: "she is woefully tedious in her narrations." No doubt she had succumbed to the garrulity of old age, but she had certainly had plenty in her life to "narrate," and a memory stored with more of interest and adventure and human relationships than most of her listeners. She ended in cheerful disillusionment and acceptance of all human limitations, finding that mankind's ceaseless scrambles after felicity

> are as childish as running after sparrows to lay salt on their tails . . . the poor efforts of our utmost prudence appearing, I fancy, in the eyes of some superior being, like the pecking of a young linnet to break a wire cage, or the climbing of a squirrel in a hoop. The moral needs no explanation: let us sing as cheerfully as we can in our impenetrable confinement, and crack our nuts with pleasure from the little store that is allowed us.

As long as she could she hid from everybody that she was dying of cancer of the breast. Her last letter was written in July 1762 and she died in August. Walpole reported in a letter in October that before her death she had "expressed great anxiety" that the two volumes of manuscript letters she had left at Rotterdam should be published. Lady Bute, however, thought otherwise. Her mother had been notorious enough during her lifetime, her brother was always in some disreputable scrape, her husband's political future and his family good name were her only interests. She wanted Lady Mary's name and her writings to be buried with her. After six months of negotiations she finally persuaded Mr. Sowden to sell her the two volumes for five hundred pounds. It must therefore have been a great shock to her to read in *The London Chronicle* a few weeks later: "This day was published the *Letters of the Right Honorable Lady M———y W———y M———u.* Mr. Sowden had to confess that one day two English gentlemen had looked at the letters and borrowed them to read at leisure. They had evidently made a copy.

Everyone except the Bute family was delighted with the letters. Edition followed edition. Smollet in the *Critical Review* declared that they were "never equalled by any letter writer of any sex, age or nationality." Another critic exclaims: "All the writer lives in every line." Voltaire thought them superior to those of Madame de Sevigné, because of their much wider scope; Dr. Johnson confessed they were the only writings he read for sheer pleasure; Edward Gibbon wrote: "What fire, what ease, what knowledge of Europe and Asia!" Even Lady Bute could not have found anything scandalous in them. But she was aware of the many other writings and letters Lady Mary had left, in particular seventeen volumes of a diary kept from the time of her marriage until the end of her life. This she decided was too inaccurate and indiscreet to survive, so she burnt it!

Lady Bute's eldest son carried on the family efforts at suppression. In 1803 he heard that a publisher, Richard Phillips, had acquired nearly two hundred private letters and was proposing to publish them. To prevent this, he bought out Phillips, with the understanding that a general authorized edition of Lady Mary's "works" should be prepared under his supervision. Meanwhile, he removed and destroyed all the letters he regarded as too personal to print. The edition, in five volumes, was full of inaccuracies. It was replaced in 1837 by an edition edited by Lord Wharncliffe, Lady Mary's great-grandson. He suppressed the "Italian Memoir," with the whole story of

Count Palazzi, and also refused to make use of the Algarotti letters. That story has been told in my introductory chapter. Lady Mary, indeed was very unlucky in the tastes of her immediate descendants, who had no liking for personal revelations. As a result, many things about her still remain dark and much of her gossip we shall never hear. Yet her longings to be remembered as a remarkable person and as an historian of her own times are amply fufilled.

# Horace Walpole

1717-1797

LESLIE STEPHEN wrote of Horace Walpole: "The history of England throughout a very large segment of the eighteenth century is simply a synonym for the works of Horace Walpole." Though this is a great simplification, it does set Walpole apart from other letter-writers. For one thing his life-span was very long. At the time of his youthful letters, Pope and Swift were still writing, and his last letters, when he was seventy-nine, were written a year before the publication of the *Lyrical Ballads* of Wordsworth and Coleridge. When the Yale edition of his correspondence, edited by Wilmarth Sheldon Lewis* is completed, it will contain some three thousand of his letters to his friends and relations and Mr. Lewis believes this represents only about forty per cent of the total he wrote. Walpole practiced various other literary pursuits and was a pioneer in several. His "Gothic" novel *The Castle of Otranto,* written in two months in 1764, was enormously popular, running into twenty-one editions before the end of the century, and at least fifty since; his blank verse tragedy *The Mysterious Mother* was also very successful. Byron referred to the two as "the first romance and the last tragedy in our language." Walpole was the first person to challenge the accepted historical picture of Richard

* By far the best introduction to the letters is the printed edition of Mr. Lewis' Mellon Lectures on Horace Walpole. Bollinger Series xxxv. Pantheon Books 1960. It has all the information needed as background, and is full of beautiful illustrations of persons and places. I am deeply indebted to it.

III in his *Historical Doubts on the Life and Reign of Richard III;* his *Aedes Walpoliana,* the description of his father's pictures, was the first book written by an Englishman on a private English collection; his five volumes, *Anecdotes of Painting in England,* compiled from the notebooks of George Vertue, are said to have "laid the foundations for an historical study of the Fine Arts in England." Besides breaking new ground in these developments, he wrote poems, pamphlets and memoirs. But his real vocation was to write letters.

He had the immense good fortune to be able to pursue his vocation without any material cares and from a position in society which made him free to meet whatever company he wished. As the younger son of Sir Robert Walpole, later Lord Orford, Prime Minister of England for over twenty years, he was born into rank and affluence. His father died when Horace was twenty-eight, leaving him a large sum of money, a house in London, and sinecure offices in the Customs. These brought him an assured income with no responsibilities, though he sat in Parliament for twenty-six years and so had a personal acquaintance with all the leading statesmen and politicians. What circumstances could be more ideal for a man of wide public, social, and cultural interests with a passion for writing letters?

He was a professional letter-writer, in the sense that he knew very well that the gift he had for it would make his "gazettes," as he called them, invaluable to future social and political historians, and he did his best to see that they were preserved. He knew that his tastes and the circumstances of his life gave him a unique opportunity to report on the many-faceted contemporary scene, and his aim was that these reports should be "accurate, truthful and entertaining." But nevertheless he was not a gazetteer but a letter-writer. Like Dorothy Osborne he declared: "I have no patience with people that don't write just as they would talk," and he thought women wrote better letters than men because by nature "they condescend to hazard a thousand trifles and negligences, which give grace, ease and familiarity to correspondence." Individuals in special fields responded to many of Walpole's particular interest: he writes especially of the political scene to Horace Mann, the English Resident in Florence; of his antiquarian interests to Thomas Cole and John Chute; of literature to Thomas Gray; of social doings and gossip and news and nonsense to country-bound friends, George Montagu, an old school-mate at Eton, and Lady Ossory, banished to retirement as the result of a divorce from her first husband, the Duke of Grafton. Yet all the letters are interwoven with personal touches, "the little circumstances of each other's society . . . the soul of letters," and with "the delicacies and attentions of friendship."

For Walpole had a genius for friendship as well as for writing letters. "When I love anybody, it is for my life," he says, and he was never guilty of "that most wicked of all sins, inconstancy." He wrote to Horace Mann for forty-five years, though they had met only once for a few weeks when he was twenty-three, and to Lady Ossory for thirty-six years. If he dropped a correspondence, as he did with George Montagu, it was because his friend dropped *him.* He published his friends' books, he promoted their careers, he entertained them at Strawberry Hill, he subscribed to their charities. He made four visits to France, though he did not care for travel, to give pleasure to poor old blind Mme. du Deffand, twenty years older than himself and who had an embarrassing infatuation for him. He wrote to her weekly for fifteen years. He had no sexual entanglements, with either men or women. He confessed that his love for his mother, who died when he was twenty, was the deepest emotion of his life, and as he observed "the vexations consequential of attachments" he had no temptation to form any:

> I own I cannot much felicitate anybody that marries for love. It is bad enough to marry: but to marry where one loves ten times worse. It is so charming at first, that the decay of inclination renders it infinitely more disagreeable afterwards.

Yet his friendships were not only constant, but deeper than he suspected. When he hears of Gray's sudden death in 1771, he writes to Chute: "I had thought that what I had seen of the world had hardened my heart; but I find that it had formed my language, not extinguished my tenderness." When Chute himself died five years later, he is heartbroken:

> Old friends are the great blessing of one's later years—half a word conveys one's meaning. They have memory of the same events, and have the same mode of thinking . . . I am lamenting my other self. Half is gone. . . . He is gone to whom I ran with every scrap of news I heard.

He breaks off his letter (to Mann), weeping, and says he must take a walk to compose himself.

But Walpole did not make the mistake of having only friends of his own age, or older. His nature was affectionate and sociable; "we are not made for solitude" he tells Montagu, urging him not to bury himself in the country. Among the children of his brother and sisters and cousins were several who were devoted to him and visited him constantly. Hannah More, some thirty years younger than himself, lived near Strawberry, and though he loved to tease her for her piety and reforming zeal, her wit and good conversation delighted him. Then, when he was seventy, Mary and Agnes Berry, both in their early twenties, came with their father to visit in the neighborhood and very soon were living in a cottage on his grounds. "The best informed and the most perfect creatures I ever saw at their age—entirely natural and unaffected, frank, and, being qualified to talk on any subject, nothing is so easy and agreeable as their conversation." Walpole called them his "dear wives" and "darling children," and since neither of them married, his final piece of good fortune was to have the last ten years of his life sweetened by their affectionate companionship.

Yet this picture of Walpole as a witty, wealthy, hospitable aristocrat, the writer of successful books, the antiquarian and collector, the possessor of long and serene friendships is a very simplified sketch of Walpole the man. The reader of the letters is, in reality, left with very mixed feelings about him. We do not grope at trying to understand him, as we do with the personality of Swift, for the letters reveal no depths of feeling nor hidden sexual drama; neither fire nor ice. He could never have experienced the ridiculous indignity of a middle-aged infatuation, like Lady Mary, nor do we feel that he ever knew any of the frustations or ecstasies or despairs of human or artistic struggle. But our responses to his personality are contradictory. Perhaps they are no different from those of his own age. Cole, the simple country vicar and antiquary, found him "one of the most lively, ingenious, and witty persons of the age," but he entered in his notebook that both Gray and himself find that Walpole's "vanity and eagerness of adulation abates and takes off from many of his shining qualities." Mason, Gray's biographer, describes him as "at times so spitfire and at times so frighted," though perhaps one should not pay too much attention to Mason, as he was a most unpleasant, egotistical man, whose vanity was never satisfied. But one of the most revealing illustrations of Walpole's conflicting impulses is his account of the government crisis of 1765. Walpole had been working actively in Parliament to bring about the fall of the ministry and to promote the fortunes of his cousin Henry Conway. The Government fell, Conway became a Secretary of State, and as Walpole wrote, not in a letter, but much later in his *Memoirs*: "I did hope that some considerable employment would be offered to me, which my vanity would have been gratified in refusing." Conway, however, told him that his name had not even been mentioned. Walpole is quite open about his not wanting any office and about the pleasure it would have been to his vanity to have refused it. He confesses to feeling "mortified" at finding that his parliamentary colleagues regarded him as a political nonentity. But the real sting was not that *they* did not mention his name, but that *Conway* didn't. He bursts out: "But what could excuse the neglect of Mr. Conway? For him I had sacrificed everything. . . . The foundations of his own fortune he owed solely to me." Wounded vanity and a sense of humiliation at a public snub were there, but they were blotted out by the feeling of a personal betrayal. And this was intensified because pride demanded that he appear to be *above* all such emotions: "I had command enough of myself not to drop a word of reproach," and in his letters of that date he ignored the episode. Yet years later all the repressed resentments were still seething as he writes the *Memoirs* for posterity.

It seems indeed as if Walpole, in both his life and his letters, had a compulsion to live up to some image he had formed of himself, and to repress aspects of his personality which conflicted with this image. He was deeply concerned with a consciousness of self, and with the impression which that self was making on other people. He reveals this very vividly in a letter to George Montagu, about a visit to his cousin, the Earl of Hertford. Walpole was forty-one at this time.

> You cannot imagine how astonished a Mr. Seward, a learned clergyman, was, who came to Ragley while I was there. Strolling about the house, he saw me first sitting on the pavement of the lumber room with Louis, all over cobwebs and dirt and mortar; then found me in his own room on a ladder writing on a picture; and half-an-hour afterwards lying on the grass in the court with the dogs and the children, in my slippers and without a hat. He had had some doubt whether I was the painter or the factotum of the family; but you would have died at his surprise when he saw me walk into dinner dressed and sit by Lady Hertford. Lord Lyttelton was there, and the conversation turned on literature: finding me not

> quite ignorant added to the parson's wonder; but he could not contain himself any longer, when after dinner he saw me go to romps and jumping with the two boys; he broke out to my Lady Hertford and begged to know who and what sort of man I really was, for he had never met with anything of the kind.

Finding out what sort of man he really was perhaps was not so important to Walpole himself as to play the part of this original, versatile aristocrat of many gifts, so dazzling to poor learned clergymen.

Much of the part was quite natural to him. He *was* original and independent in spirit. In his youth he had a fund of what he called "natural ferocity and wildness," which made him impatient of the dull social restraints of his father's house. At a time when travelers spoke of the "high and hideous Alps," Walpole wrote ecstatically to his young friend Richard West of the beauties among the Savoy mountains:

> The road, West, the road! winding round a prodigious mountain, and surrounded with others, all shagged with hanging woods, obscured with pines, or lost in clouds! . . . Sheets of cascades forcing their silver speed down channelled precipices, and hasting into the roughened river at the bottom! Now and then an old footbridge, with a broken rail, a leaning cross, a cottage, or the ruin of an hermitage! . . .

He is afraid West will think him "too bombast and romantic," but Walpole was born with a strong romantic strain in him. As an undergraduate at Cambridge he "doated" on its antiquities, and the loveliness of King's College Chapel "penetrated me with a visionary longing to be a monk in it." Delight in the "gothic" was implanted in him from that time, and when he became independent after his father's death, and wanted a country house of his own, he bought a cottage at Twickenham called Strawberry Hill and proceeded to turn it into a sham Gothic castle. Strawberry hill was Walpole's consuming life-interest, and it too reflects different aspects of his strangely conflicting personality. He loved its country beauties: "set in enamelled meadows, with filigree hedges"; he delighted in the garden scents on a June night:

> The acacias, which the Arabians had the sense to worship, are covered in blossoms, the honeysuckles dangle from every tree in festoons, the seringas are thickets of sweets, and the new cut hay in the meadow tempers the balmy gales with simple freshness.

It was also a literary retreat where he could house and build up a fine library and establish his private printing press for his own works and those of his friends.

In the house itself, however, and in much of its contents, the romantic "wildness" in his nature expressed itself in an extraordinary mixture of the genuine and the shoddy, and the "ferocity" in the crude pursuit of possessions to furnish his "castle" according to his taste. Though he had a genuine, instinctive love of the medieval and really launched the "Gothic revival" by inspiring antiquarians to explore the realities of Gothic architecture, it was characteristic of Walpole that he never studied the subject himself in any workmanlike way. It did not offend his taste that his castle should be a fake imitation, decorated with lath and plaster pinnacles and battlements, and wall-paper painted in perspective to look like carved stone. He wanted it to convey "the gloomth of abbeys and cathedrals" and was happy with his dark entrances, gingerbread cloisters, and niches filled with alleged medieval trophies. He traveled all over England "casting a Gothic eye" on antiquities. This frequently meant persuading impoverished churches or householders to sell him their stained glass, pictures, carvings, or statuary. He crammed the rooms with pictures, prints, miniatures, enamels, snuffboxes, china, and glass, old and new. Though later, Strawberry became so popular that the constant stream of visitors was a nuisance—he wrote in 1786: "my house is a torment not a comfort"—at first his greatest delight was to show off his treasures. It is perhaps as the genial host that we picture him most vividly: a short, lean figure, with high forehead, long, pale face and bright dark eyes. He had a mincing walk, but wore no hat or overcoat, having a great belief in fresh air, and hardening the constitution. The printing press would welcome friends with a copy of complimentary verses; on the terrace was the blue and white china tub in which Gray's "pensive Selima" gazed at the goldfish and discovered, in death, that all that glitters is not gold. Inside was the chapel, with its entire window bought from a church at Bexhill; all his really valuable pictures and books and bibelots, along with such alleged "relics" as Cardinal Wolsey's red hat, a comb belonging to Mary, Queen of Scots, and the spurs worn by William III at the Battle of the Boyne.

Walpole's collections and publications brought him fame, but again his response was ambiguous; he both welcomed and enjoyed admiration, and was yet ever ready to play down his own performance. Part of this was true modesty: "For talents, what are mine, but trifling and superficial; and compared with those of men of real genius, most diminutive." At the same time he despised scholarship and was impatient with experts who pointed out his errors. He told Gray that he could not be bothered to revise or correct his work: "If I write tolerably it must be at once; I can neither mend nor add." To his aristocratic friends he is more outspoken, remarking that professionalism in scholarship is only "having read more foolish books than other folk," while "minute accuracy" is fit only for "microscopic intellects." His ideal is to be a "polite author," who does not want to be thought serious; he is the talented amateur who takes no pains over his productions, and whose work has "all the beautiful negligence of a gentleman."

This accounts perhaps for his negative responses to the literature of his own time. Walpole was an extremely well-read man. His letters are full of quotations and allusions to the writings of the past, yet he failed to appreciate any of the great figures of his own age. It is true that the age was not rich in poets; his comment "Pope and poetry are dead," had some validity. We forgive his belief that Gray was a major poet, since that was colored by personal friendship, and it was natural that he should have enjoyed Chatterton and Macpherson's Ossian. Their imitations of antiquity matched his own "Gothic" taste, and he was not scholar enough to detect that the poems were forgeries. Perhaps too he was right to dismiss Goldsmith as "piddling," and it is probable that he never heard of Burns or Blake, though he gives a kind word to Crabbe. But it is his dismissal of the prose writers which betrays his inability to recognize any robust vitality or psychological insight, and his isolation from the true literary genius and accomplishment of his time. "What a figure will this Augustan Age make!" he exclaims, and indeed it does in his criticism. He admired the first volume of Gibbon's *Decline and Fall*, but found the author ridiculously vain, and enjoyed trying to deflate him. When Gibbon lent him the second volume he commented on returning it that the subject was so "disgusting" that he was afraid "few will have patience to read it." When Gibbon colored at this insult and stammered out: "It had never been put together before," Walpole adds: "So *well* he meant to add." He then dismisses book and author: "So much for literature and its fops." The novels of Richardson are "a mere picture of high life as conceived by a bookseller"; those of Fielding "perpetually disgusting"; *Tristram Shandy* "the dregs of nonsense," and Smollett "a most worthless and dangerous fellow." It is natural that Dr. Johnson's bad manners should have repelled Walpole's fastidiousness, but he sees nothing beyond them: "a saucy Caliban with a fustian style and a mean spirit, who behaves like an ill-natured bear, and in opinion is as senseless a bigot as an old washerwoman." What an age, when London welcomes literary sketches of this mountebank by "that ridiculous woman," Mrs. Piozzi, and "that quintessence of busybodies," James Boswell!

Such opinions, and other spurts of prejudice, make us suspect that Walpole, under his pose of aristocratic superiority, was no more free than most of us from hidden resentments and feelings of anxiety and inadequacy. It may well be, as Mr. Lewis suggests, that his gout was a physical expression of these emotional stresses. But that at times "the beautiful negligence of a gentleman" became a defensive mask to cover these common weaknesses does not mean that there was no genuine humanity beneath it. Walpole could not have written his letters with the freshness and zest they possess had he really been, as Macaulay said, "a heartless fribble," with a mind full of "inconstant whims and affectations," and features "covered by mask within mask." He could be as kind as he was malicious. He gave a home at Strawberry to two poor old women; one an illegitimate half-sister, and the other an old friend, of his mother; he loved children, and apologizes to Conway for cancelling a visit to him because of the presence of a little girl who is sick: "You know how courteous a knight I am to distrest virgins of five years old, and that my castle gates are always open to them." He was devoted to his pets and had a succession of beloved dogs, "dear, good-natured, honest, sensible creatures." Even if one has none of these qualities, he will not repudiate it. When Mme. du Deffand died, he took her unpleasant little lap-dog, Tonton: "which is so cross, that I am sure nobody else would treat it well." On arrival at Strawberry, Tonton first chased Walpole's favorite cat out of the room and then flew at one of the other dogs. He settled down, however, and survived, "by constant attention," until at the age of sixteen, stone-deaf and nearly blind, he died, "close by my side, without a pang or a groan." Walpole was beloved by all his servants, and was "partial to all youth." He hated blood sports and war, and years before any great public outcry at the slave trade he exclaimed: "It chills one's blood."

All these contradictory aspects of Walpole's character come out in the letters and are part of their fascination, but what he was consciously trying to do in his correspondence was to create a memorable first-hand account of contemporary personalities, society and public events. He knew no one was better qualified than he to do this. He writes in 1785, when he was sixty-eight:

> I kissed the hand of George I and am now hearing the frolics of his great great grandson . . . I have seen a mistress of James II, the Duke of Marlborough's funeral, three or four wars, the whole career, victories and death of Lord Chatham, the loss of America. . . . Then for private episodes, varieties of character, political intrigues, literary anecdotes etc., the profusion I remember is endless.

In the letters we live through these not as memories but as elements surrounding Walpole's daily life as he passes from youth to old age. We meet him first as a youth doing the Grand Tour, a brilliant young man of fashion who quarrels with his serious and impecunious companion, Gray, but is also disgusted with the immaturity of most of the young men he meets. He loves "the inanimate part" of Rome and all "glorious desolate prospects," but has none of Lady Mary's delight in new places and experiences for their own sakes. Indeed he never went abroad again except to Paris, and never very far from Strawberry and London in England.

We have a glimpse of him electioneering in King's Lynn, in Norfolk, addressing "the mob" in the Town Hall, and then "riding at the head of 2000 people . . . dining with above 200 of them, amid bumpers, huzzas, soup and tobacco, and finishing with country dances at a ball and sixpenny whist." He declares he has borne it all cheerfully, but we feel he is very much more at home at the King's Birthday Ball, in a new Paris suit, and reporting to his cousin afterwards: "My Aunt Horace had adapted her gown to her complexion, and chose a silk all broke out in pink blotches"; or at an evening party at Vauxhall with Lady Caroline Petersham, "looking gloriously jolly and handsome," stewing seven minced chickens in a china dish over a lamp with 3 pats of butter and a flagon of water, "stirring and rattling and laughing"; such a cheerful party, indeed that they don't get home till three o'clock in the morning. Another cheerful episode, in retrospect, was the embarrassing comedy of situation on an outing at Strawberry in June 1756. Walpole describes it to Lord Strafford:

> My Lady Ailesbury, Mr Conway and Miss Rich passed two days last week at Strawbwerry Hill. We were returning from Mrs Clive's through the long field, and had got over the high stile that comes into the road; that is, three of us. It had rained and the stile was wet. I could not let Miss Rich straddle across so damp a palfrey, but took her in my arms to lift her over. At that instant I saw a coach and six come thundering down the hill from my house; and hurrying to set down my charge, and stepping backwards, I missed the first step, came down headlong with the nymph in my arms; but turning quite round as we rushed to the ground, the first thing that touched the earth was Miss Rich's head. You must guess in how improper a situation we fell; and you must not tell my lady Strafford before anybody that every petticoat, etc. in the world were canted—high enough indeed! The coach came on and never stopped. The apprehension that it would run over my Chloe made me lie where I was. . . . The ladies, who were Lady Holdernesse, Miss Pelham and your sister Lady Mary Coke, stared with astonishment at the theatre which they thought I had chosen to celebrate our loves; the footmen laughed; and you may imagine the astonishment of Mr Conway and Lady Ailesbury, who did not see the fall, but turned and saw our attitude. It was these spectators that amazed Miss Pelham, who described the adventure to Mrs Pitt, and said, "What was most amazing, there were Mr Conway and Lady Ailesbury looking on!

"There is nothing so pleasant in a letter as the occurrences of society," he writes, and he seems to miss very few of them at this time. Anything that "makes a buzz" is food for his pen. He sees Blenheim: "it looks like the palace of an auctioneer," and goes to the first night at Ranelagh Gardens, the new open-air night-club, with dancing, illuminations, music, supper-parties and gaming tables; tells of the arrival from Ireland and the subsequent fortunes of the two beautiful Gunning sisters, "who make more noise than any of their predecessors since the days of Helen"; the doings of the bigamist Maid of Honour, Miss Chudleigh; a glimpse of the Duchess of Queensberry, noted for the bizarre in dress, who appeared at court in a gown and petticoat of red flannel; and the runaway match of Lord Ilchester's daughter with an actor: "which is indeed the completion of disgrace—even a footman were preferable; the publicity of the hero's profession perpetuates the mortification." We hear Lady Coventry (Maria Gunning), confiding innocently to old King George II that the one thing she longs to see is a Coronation; and how the Sunday before the hanging of a notorious highwayman, three thousand ladies and gentlemen crowded to look at him in his cell at Newgate; and how a further illustration of the frivolous temper of the times is that "my Lord Rockingham and my nephew Lord Orford have made a match of £500 between 5 turkeys and 5 geese to run from Norwich to London."

He goes to see the new actor, David Garrick: "nothing very wonderful," he comments, though it is heresy to say so, and heresy not to admire "the insufferable nonsense he writes about Shakespeare"; he gives some rather grudging admiration to Mrs. Siddons, and reports a vogue for Peg Woffington: "a bad actress, but she has life." We hear of the popularity of Pantomime; of Handel's success in making oratories more fashionable than operas, though, says Walpole "they give me an idea of Heaven where everybody is to sing, whether they have voices or not." Then the eclipse of Handel by Glück, riots in the theatre about the high price of seats; a scene at Drury Lane when the gallery stood up and shouted "Wilkes and Liberty" when the King was in his box; and the first performance by amateur actors, "people of some quality" at Drury Lane. Besides amateur acting, another new vogue is amateur painting, as well as the fashion—created so largely by Walpole himself—for private collections of china and prints. He believes that these tastes are going to make the old women of the next generation so much more agreeable, since they will have amusements outside cards and scandal.

In 1790, he notes what seems to have been a beatnik phase in fashion: "the dirty shirts and shaggy hair of the young men . . . have confounded all individuality." But by then he was an old man and was suffering from the common belief of the old that manners and morals have degenerated. He thinks the pomp of Garrick's funeral "perfectly ridiculous," even shameful: "What distinction remains for the patriot hero, when the most solemn have been showered on a player?" He lashes out at the news hounds of the gutter press: "they now call it a *duty* to publish all these calamities which decency to wretched relations used in compassion to suppress." He notes the shocking violence growing among the lower classes: "But no wonder—how should the morals of the people be purified when such frantic dissipation reigns above them?" "Frenzy, folly, extravagance and insensibility are everywhere. Hours get later and later, and though London has more public diversions than would suffice for two capitals, nobody goes to them till they are over, since it has become the fashion never to be punctual."

Walpole concludes this diatribe, in a letter to Mann in 1782:

> Well! but is not this censure being old and cross? Were not the charming people of my youth guilty of equivalent absurdities? Oh yes; but the sensible folks of my youth had not lost America, nor dipped us in wars with half Europe, that cost us fifteen millions a year . . .

We hear as much in the letters of the doings of the so-called "sensible folks" as we do of the small change of "society," and view all the outstanding historical events of the time as they appeared to an educated contemporary. Walpole, as a Whig, had no sympathy for the Jacobites, yet he appreciated the courage of many of the rebel leaders of 1745 under trial and execution. He justly condemns the conviction of Admiral Byng, shot for cowardice and treason in 1757 because the Navy wanted a scapegoat for the mismanagement of the war against the French. Walpole's description of his death is very moving:

> A few days before, one of his friends standing by him, said, "Which of us is tallest?" He replied, "Why this ceremony? I know what it means; let the man come and measure me for my coffin." . . . He desired to be shot on the quarter-deck, not where common malefactors are; came out at twelve, sat down on a chair, for he would not kneel, and refused to have his face covered, that his countenance might show whether he feared death; but being told that it might frighten his executioners, he submitted, gave the signal at once, received one shot through the head, another through the heart, and fell. Do cowards live or die thus?

We hear of the death of the notorious Frederick, Prince of Wales; and then of his father George II; and in a fine vein of grotesque comedy, follow the behavior of the mad old Duke of Newcastle at the King's funeral:

> He fell into a fit of crying as soon as he came into the chapel, and flung himself back in a stall, the Archbishop hovering over him with a smelling bottle: but in two minutes his curiosity got the better of his hypocrisy, and he ran about the chapel with his glass, to spy who was or was not there, spying with one hand and mopping his eyes with the other. Then returned the fear of catching cold; and the Duke of Cumberland, who was sinking with heat, felt himself weighed down, and turning round, found it was the Duke of Newcastle standing on his train, to avoid the chill of the marble.

Though Walpole made no mark in Parliament himself, it was natural that his father's son should have a keen eye for the political figures of the age, and they throng the pages of his letters. Lord Hervey is there, with his "coffin face," an elder brother of Lady Mary's friend, an associate of Sir Robert Walpole himself, and, some whispered, lover of Lady Walpole and true father of Horace. We watch the career of the elder Pitt, Lord Chatham, to that scene in the House of Lords, where in the middle of a speech defending the American colonists, he collapsed and "fell down in an apoplectic fit." We have many glimpses of that most magnificent of rakes and wits and gamblers and politicians—Charles James Fox. Walpole saw him, after his five-hour speech for the prosecution at the trial of Warren Hastings, handing ladies into their coaches "with all the gaiety and prattle of an idle gallant"; and listened to him on another occasion when, after returning from the races at Newmarket, and gambling at Almacks the whole night through, Fox went straight to the House of Commons and held it spellbound by the brilliance of his oratory. We see England under a Prime Minister, the Duke of Grafton, who "thinks the world should be postponed to a horse race," watch the mediocre, muddling Lord Bute, Lady Mary's son-in-law, and feel impotently all that appalling series of blunders by which England lost America.

From the beginning all Walpole's sympathies were with the colonists: "our conduct has been that of pert children: we have thrown a pebble at a mastiff, and are surprised that it was not frightened." He rejoiced that the outcome means "that there is still a great continent of Englishmen who will remain free and independent," and he loves "to skip into futurity and imagine what will be done on the giant scale of a new hemisphere." No one would have been happier than Walpole to know that the editor-in-chief of his complete correspondence and the foremost collector of Walpoliana is an American.

Walpole's view of European affairs and England's destiny became darker and darker. In 1784 he declared "Mr. Pitt is certainly an extraordinary young man; but is he a supernatural one?" and in spite of Pitt's successes, he continued to see the country "on the verge of ruin." England was "quarrelling with all Europe," the whole political world in a state of "shameless corruption," and the "sottish, stupid nation" so decayed from its days of greatness under his father that in a couple of generations she may well be a mere province of France.

When he had first visited France in 1765, he had enjoyed his own popularity and the good company of Mme. du Deffand and other *salonistes.* But he thought little of Parisian houses and gardens, music and theatres, compared with those of London, and was horrified at the neglect of the pictures in the Louvre, in Versailles and in private houses. The conscientious atheism of the "philosophes" and of the whole fashionable community offended his taste and sense of decorum. Though he could write privately: "Church and presbytery are human nonsense invented by knaves to govern fools," his opinion is strongly that "Freethinking is for oneself, surely not for society," and he is shocked at an open discussion of the Bible at a dinner-table, "though all the servants were waiting." He would not have permitted it at his own table, he says, "if a single footman was present." In literary circles, the popularity of David Hume and Samuel Richardson amazes him, and he considered Rousseau "an affected mountebank." His later visits contrast the gay brilliance of the Court against the mounting national bankruptcy and the sufferings of the poor, and on his last trip in 1775, although the beauty of the young Queen, Marie Antoinette, dazzled him, he recognized the mixture of parade and poverty everywhere hand in hand, and leaves the country "as peevish as if I were posterity."

While the American revolution had filled him with admiration of the rebels, and he hated the exploitation of any subject people—"Who but Machiavel can pretend that we have a shadow of title to a foot of land in India?"—yet the French revolution filled him with horror. "No man is more devoted to liberty than I am; yet blood is a terrible price to pay for it." Nevertheless, he does not blame the mobs who took over nearly as much as the leaders who set it in motion, who "seem to think they can entirely new-model the world with metaphysical compasses," and "who proceed in rending all ties and overturning all systems, without repairing or replacing any."

By this time Walpole was an old man and as disillusioned about human nature in general as Swift himself:

> I am not surprised at the idea of the devil being always at our elbows. They who invented him no doubt could not conceive how men could be so atrocious to one another, without the intervention of a fiend.

It is the same with the inventions of man's hands and minds. Walpole sees very clearly where the conquest of the air will end. He comments on the discovery of the balloon:

> Well! I hope these new mechanic meteors will prove only playthings for the learned and the idle, and not be converted into new engines of destruction to the human race, as is so often the case of refinements or discoveries in science. The wicked wit of man always studies to apply the result of talents to enslaving, destroying, or cheating his fellow-creatures. Could we reach the moon, we should think of reducing it to a province of some European kingdom.

He sets himself resolutely however, to count his personal blessings and to look at himself objectively: "I know that an angry old man out of Parliament, and that can do nothing but be angry, is a ridiculous animal." His attacks of "that venomous devil," the gout, steadily increased in severity. He bore them with whimsical fortitude, had a healthy distrust of contemporary medicine and relied for relief on the popular "James's Powders," the aspirin of the day. Walpole had trusted to "great abstinence" to keep the gout away, but found however, that "virtue and leanness," his Spartan hardening regimes of cold water inside and out, were all alike useless. Damp naturally affected him badly and the English climate was as it always has been. "One must have seen such a thing as spring," he writes one April, "or one could not have invented the idea"; we read of forty-eight hours of incessant rain in mid-June, so that "my poor hay has not a dry thread on its back," and of the same season twenty-two years later when "hay and ice, orange-flowers and rheumatisms" keep one another company. He dates a letter "the first of July and consequently the middle of winter," and cowering over a fire, remarks that in an English summer "the best sun we have is made of Newcastle coal." Six months before his death, though he was then quite crippled and had to be carried about by two servants, he can still recognize "vast blessings." He has preserved his eyes, ears and teeth, and can outsleep any dormouse. His thoughts go out to "the thousands of old poor, who are suffering martyrdom," and have none of the reliefs and comforts that he can pay for.

In 1766, Walpole wrote to George Montagu that in some volumes of Swift's correspondence just published is "his own journal sent to Stella during the 4 last years of the Queen." Though Walpole had the greatest contempt for Swift's personality and Tory politics, he found the Journal "a fund of entertainment. . . . What strikes one, is bringing before one's eyes the incidents of a curious period." Or again he writes of the letters of his beloved Mme. de Sevigné: "She has the art of making you acquainted with all her acquaintance and attaches you even to spots she inhabited"; and that "when her mind is full of any great event, she interests you with the warmth of a dramatic writer, not with the chilly impartiality of an historian." No one could accuse Walpole of impartiality, but it is neither his enthusiasms nor his prejudices which mainly concern us. It is his capacity to create the living moment at which he is writing, and to surround it with so much of his own personality. Perhaps he hides as much as he reveals; he had none of the modern taste for self-analysis and introspecton; perhaps indeed, there were no depths to explore. What he gives us is an unfading relish for talking on paper to his various friends and relations about everything that happens to him and everything that he hears and everything that his own mind creates. Seldom has anyone had such a span of interest and experiences and topics: politics, wars, revolutions, parties, society gossip, Strawberry, books, pictures, plays, memories, anecdotes, dogs, visitors, fashions. The subject matter is endless and he could present it all and weave it together, with clarity and good sense, with warmth and wit, with sentiment or cynicism. We may not feel the human affection and sympathy for him that we feel for some other letter-writers, but he is the best company in the world.

# William Cowper

1731-1800

WILLIAM COWPER'S name is not mentioned in the letters of Horace Walpole. Walpole was one of the subscribers to Cowper's translation of Homer, and since Hannah More was so enthusiastic about *The Task,* she must have tried to get him to read it. It is unlikely, however, that that epic of cosy domesticity and country occupations and simple piety would appeal to the sophisticated Walpole. Indeed it would be impossible to find two personalities more different than these two men who were almost exact contemporaries, and both of whom live because of their letters; or two kinds of living more different than those revealed in their correspondence. They inhabit completely different worlds; Walpole traveled, dilettante, dandified, never outside the atmosphere of wealthy ease; spending his time among ministers of state, aristocrats, antiquarians, wealthy wits and rakes, titled older women or young ones winning or sinning their way to riches or rank. Cowper who never even had a study of his own, and who spent his time among country clergymen, schoolmasters, and the minor "gentry." Hardly a name among his correspondents lives in either history or literature. Walpole was writing deliberately for posterity, whether he is telling of parliamentary conflicts, or literary reputations or spicy scandals; while Cowper recorded for his personal friends his simple daily life in a Buckinghamshire village, deliberately anchoring himself in trivialities to avoid the terror of madness. Yet his very smallness of scope has its charm, and his writing has a spontaneity and elegance and humor which has its own special flavor.

Cowper could boast as good a family as Walpole. His father, a country clergyman, came of a line of distinguished lawyers and politicians and churchmen. His mother was a Donne, tracing her lineage back to the famous poet and beyond. But his father's family had a heritage of nervous instability and Cowper was its victim. Some of his biographers blame his mental troubles on his conversion to Evangelicanism and its emotional extravagances, but it seems more probable that religious mania was simply the form in which his psychic disturbance manifested itself. Whatever its origin, it blighted his life. He became, as he said "an irreclaimable hermit," from the age of thirty-three. Although, after the publication of *The Task* in 1785, Cowper was perhaps the most popular English poet for the next fifty years, all his writing, like his other hobbies, was in the nature of occupational therapy. They all helped him temporarily to escape his conflicts; they did nothing to resolve them. No one knew better than himself that his art was of the surface only: he said he had no more right to the name of poet "than a maker of mousetraps has to that of an engineer," and he was quite unable to find any true creative release in exploring the hidden depths of his own despair.

"A poor fly, entangled in a thousand webs from the beginning," is how he saw himself; but it was not quite from the beginning. It is true that the death of his mother at his brother's birth, when Cowper was six years old, was a terrible blow to the sensitive child. The sudden withdrawal of "the constant flow of love that knew no fall" was such a shock that he remembered every detail of it forty-seven years later. It is quite possible that this loss of loving security, followed by a period of brutal bullying by a boy ten years older than himself at a boarding school, may have implanted a terror of rejection and the sense of helplessness before apparent omnipotence. But he was removed from the school because of weak eyes and put in charge of a kindly oculist, where he stayed until at ten years old he was sent to Westminster School, which then ranked next to Eton in fame. Though later Cowper wrote a long poem attacking the harsh brutalities of the fashionable schools of the time, strangely enough he seems to have been quite happy at Westminster. He won a prize for Latin verses, developed a love of Greek, enjoyed playing cricket and football, and made many friends. On leaving, however, his lifelong incapacity to make any choices for himself led him to acquiesce in his father's decision that he should study law. It was an unfortunate choice, since Cowper had no interest whatever in the subject, nor any ambition to make a career in that profession.

He spent three years in an attorney's office, then took chambers in the Temple, and was called to the Bar in 1754, when he was twenty-three. But during these years and for some time after, he seems to have lived a gay and happy life as a gifted drifter, supported by his father and spending most of his time at the house of his well-to-do uncle, Ashley Cowper, and in the society of his two daughters, Harriot and Theodora, and their circle of young friends. These included James Thurlow, later Lord Chancellor, and Joseph Hill, an attorney who became wealthy and who proved a faithful friend and financial benefactor to Cowper throughout his life: "an unreserved acceptance of what is graciously offered is the handsomest way of dealing with one of your character," wrote Cowper, some thirty years later. It was fortunate for him that there was always someone of that "character" to help in need. Meanwhile he became engaged to his cousin Theodora, was a member of a cheerful and witty group of young men who called themselves the Nonsense Club, wrote verses, essays, reviews, translations, danced and went to the theater and opera. A letter from one of the members of the Club published in *The Gentleman's Magazine* in 1786, when Cowper was famous as the author of *The Task,* praised him especially as a brilliant talker, "with the extraordinary power of being ludicrous whenever he pleased."

Cowper had had a short spell of pathological depression when he first went to live in the Temple in 1723, but it had been lightened by reading the poetry of George Herbert and a happy visit to the country near Southampton, where, in the beautiful surroundings, "I felt the weight of all my misery taken off." In a memoir found among his papers after his death, which is our only source of knowledge for his second breakdown ten years later, he has convinced himself that it was "a neglect to improve the mercies of God at Southampton" that was a sin against the Holy Ghost. There were other factors, however, which may have contributed. By then his younger brother had proved himself a brilliant linguist and classical scholar, and had been elected to a Fellowship at Cambridge; his friends were scattering to their various careers; his cousin Harriot was married to Sir Thomas Hesketh and had left London; and Ashley Cowper, since his nephew had no prospects and had already shown signs of mental instability, had insisted that his engagement to Theodora should be ended. His father too had died and he was in need of money.

It seemed a very fortunate chance that a Clerkship to the House of Lords fell vacant, and that a cousin with political influence was willing to nominate Cowper for the post, which would have meant financial independence for life. He discovered, however, that there were to be other nominees, and that the outcome would be decided by an oral examination at the Bar of the House. It would seem that Cowper must already have been on the way to breakdown. He was an easy speaker and good scholar, and it is incredible that in normal circumstances he would have any dread of answering a few questions on material that he had plenty of time to prepare. But he became overwhelmed with a sense of panic. A few days before the examination his terror drove him to some inefficient efforts at suicide. But someone was watching when he planned to drown himself; he found he could not drink the laudanum he bought; his penknife broke when he tried stabbing, and the garter snapped when he attempted hanging. It was clear that he could not attend the examination, but the next phase of his disorder was to be overwhelmed with a sense of sin at having tried to take his own life. He was tormented by a dream in which he tried to join in a service at Westminster Abbey, and the iron gates of the choir clanged in his face. He could not remember the words of the creed and lay "howling with horror." The "uproar within" drowned out all communication with friends and relatives and he was removed to the home of a Dr. Cotton in St. Albans where he stayed for eighteen months. It was here that under the influence of the doctor, who was an enthusiastic Evangelical, he had the sense of release that had visited him before in Southampton, though this time he attributes it directly to divine grace. He writes to his cousin Harriot:

> My affliction has taught me a road to happiness which without it I should never have found; and I know, and have experience of it every day, that the mercy of God, to him who believes himself the object of it, is more than sufficient to compensate for the loss of every other blessing.

Cowper was ready to leave Dr. Cotton's home in May 1765, and his brother at Cambridge suggested that he should find lodgings in Huntington nearby. One suspects that young John Cowper did not want his company in Cambridge itself. His own religious views were strictly orthodox and he was very distrustful of his brother's new "enthusiasm." A few lonely months followed for Cowper. Humorously he reports on his total incapacity to cope with practical matters, such as housekeeping, servants, or living within his small allowance. (Though he seems to believe this is his own money, it seems more probable that it came from Joseph Hill and his uncle.) Then he had the good fortune to make friends with the Unwin family. The father was a scholarly old clergyman, the mother much younger, a very intelligent and sympathetic woman; the son, destined also for the Church, was an undergraduate at Cambridge, and the daughter still a child. Soon Cowper was spending most of his time there: "Go when I will, I find a house filled with peace and cordiality in all its parts." The family is "altogether the cheerfulest and most engaging it is possible to conceive." As for Mrs. Unwin: "that woman is a blessing to me, and I never see her without being the better for her company."

A few months later, the Unwins invited Cowper to make his home with them, and he was blissfully contented in a quiet routine of Bible-reading, hymn-singing, church services, letter-writing, riding, gardening, and walking and talking with Mrs. Unwin: "I am cheerful and happy, and having peace with God, have peace with myself." He has a passing thought of taking orders himself, but adds: "They who have had the least idea of what I have suffered from the dread of public exhibition, will readily excuse my never attempting it hereafter." He had indeed really abdicated all thought of taking responsibility for his own life, and slipped into complete emotional and practical dependence upon the Unwins. Two years later, however, in 1767, Mr. Unwin was killed by a fall from his horse. This meant a removal from the Huntington parsonage, and fate arranged it that they should meet the Reverend John Newton, curate at the small town of Olney in Buckinghamshire. Newton, who as a young man had been a convinced atheist, had had a most varied and adventurous career. Press-ganged into the Navy, he had later worked on West African plantations, and been captain of a slave ship. He had survived incredible hardships and dangers, but on his return to England had been "converted," had met both Wesley and Whitefield, and finally took orders in the Church of England. He threw himself into his new career with immense energy and enthusiasm; was determined that the Unwins and Cowper should settle at Olney and help him with his work; and three months later they were there.

The only house available, Orchard Side, their home for the next nineteen years, was most ugly and unattractive. (Renovated, it is now the Cowper and Newton Museum.) It was badly built, damp and drafty, with "a parlor that looks the north wind full in the face." The front door opened on to a noisy and dirty market-place, and its only recommendation was that its narrow strip of garden at the back adjoined that of the vicarage. It was altogether a sad change from Huntington, and not only were the physical surroundings so different, but all the peaceful serenity of that happy life was shattered by Newton's dynamic fanaticism. He lived in a whirl of preaching, writing, visiting the sick, leading prayer-meetings and teaching Bible classes, and he urged Cowper to join in all these activities. Cowper was hypnotized by all this abounding vitality, but quite incapable of responding at such a pitch and pace of ecstatic dedication. He began to feel periods of spiritual stagnation and deprivation. In 1770 the illness and death of his young brother shocked and grieved him, and shortly after this Newton suggested to Cowper that he should marry Mrs. Unwin, only seven years his senior. Her daughter was engaged to be married and would shortly be leaving their home. Cowper, whose devotion to Mary Unwin was purely filial, and who shrank from taking any responsibility anyhow, was horrified at the idea, and it seems as if his revulsion from the thought of it helped to plunge him again into complete breakdown. It was probably responsible too for all the later gossip that Cowper suffered from a sexual deformity. After Cowper's death, Newton let it be known that the poet had confessed to him that he could not marry because he was a hermaphrodite. It seems quite certain that if Cowper did believe this, and used it as a reason against marriage with Mrs. Unwin, it was simply a delusion, and part of his psychotic condition at the time. Southey, the first editor of Cowper, suppressed all mention of it, being convinced that it was such: "If the fact had been as he supposed, it was not merely unlikely, but absolutely impossible that he should ever have been sent to a public school—or to any boarding school." Not only that, which is a strong enough argument, but the fact that he had been engaged happily for two years to his cousin Theodora seems to make the suggestion absurd.

The mental and emotional derangement that struck him in 1773 brought all the raving terrors of ten years earlier. He was moved to the vicarage where Newton and his wife and Mrs. Unwin cared for him devotedly, but it was sixteen months before he and Mrs. Unwin moved back to Orchard Side. No further talk of marriage ever arose. Cowper had emerged from his first bad attack into the joy and assurance of salvation, but he emerged from the second with the unalterable conviction of damnation. He had had a dream in which God's voice had said: "it is all over with thee: thou hast perished." Thenceforth Cowper was a dual personality. His spiritual existence was a night-life of terrible dreams and an abiding consciousness of abandonment by his God; his outward behavior was a daily struggle to hide his condition and to escape from it by constant physical or mental activity. Since he was convinced that he had forever forfeited God's mercy, he made no pretense of religious observance, refused to go to church, or even to say a grace before meals. He was equally certain that no prayers by others on his behalf would be listened to. It was useless for the robust and practical Newton to appeal to his common sense:

> How strange that your judgment should be clouded on one point only, and that a point so obvious and strikingly clear to every body who knows you! . . . I know not that I ever saw you for a single day since your calamity came upon you, in which I could not perceive as clear and satisfying evidence that the Grace of God was with you as I could in your brighter and happier times.

Cowper's replies to such comfort were always the same: "He who once loved me now hates me"; or "He has rejected me finally, and all promises and all answers to prayers made for me are mere delusions."

> The weather is an exact emblem of my mind. . . . A thick fog envelopes everything, and at the same time it freezes intensely. You will tell me that this cold gloom will be succeeded by a cheerful spring . . . but it will be lost labour. Nature revives again; but a soul once slain lives no more.

To the argument that such treatment of him would be unworthy of a loving God, he counters: "He is the fittest judge of what is worthy of him," and when he feels that he cannot reasonably resist the assurances of the Gospels, he falls back upon the position that he is unique: "There is no encouragement in the Scriptures so comprehensive as to include my case, nor any consolation so effective as to reach it." He is "plunged in depths unvisited, I am convinced, by any human soul than mine," and "I have never met, either in books or in conversation, with an experience at all similar."

Cowper's living nightmare of emotional torture hardly bears thinking of. Sometimes it is a simple cry of pain: "You will think me mad, but I am not mad . . . I am only in despair." Sometimes his sense of doom provokes a vivid analogy: he is "in the belly of this hell, compared with which Jonah's was a Paradise." The winter months especially are filled with terrors:

> I know the ground before I tread upon it; it is hollow, it is agitated, it suffers shock in every direction; it is like the soil of Calabria, all whirlpool and undulation; but I must reel through it—at least if I be not swallowed up by the way.

All the rest of Cowper's life was played out against this background, but fortunately, outside his fixed obsession, his mind was quite rational, his temperament gentle and lovable, and he had the gift for giving tender, constant affection, and inspiring it in others. He declared that he was unlike the usual type of melancholic: "I have not that which commonly is a symptom of such a case . . . extraordinary elevation in the absence of Mr. Bluedevil," yet partly through his own determination to occupy himself and to ignore the curse upon him, and partly through the stimulus which a succession of new friends brought into his life, he had many periods of quiet productive happiness. He speaks of his "valor of a passive kind," in "the arduous task of being merry by force," and putting on "an air of cheerfulness and vivacity to which I am in reality a stranger"; but he manages most successfully to make it all sound spontaneous. The loving companionship of Mary Unwin was his constant human prop; he had a passionate love of nature: "I can look at the same rivulet, or at a handsome tree, every day of my life, with new pleasure"; and for the first two years after his recovery, he filled his days with various forms of "physical therapy": gardening, carpentry, cabinet-making, drawing. A neighbor gave him a tame hare; it was soon joined by two more, and by goldfish, guinea-pigs, birds, cats and dogs. The hymns he and Newton had composed before his breakdown were published in 1779, and now, as in his early years, he wrote occasional verse on light topics and eight Satires on moral qualities.

And he started to write long letters again, though as he points out with humorous irony, he has little time for them:

> My mornings engrossed by the garden; and in the afternoon, till I have drunk tea, I am fit for nothing. At five we walk, and when the walk is over, lassitude recommends rest, and again I become fit for nothing.

Moreover Olney is not a hotbed of news: "No place contributes less to the catalogue of incidents, or is more scantily supplied with anecdotes worth notice." But Cowper has an enchanting gift of making fun out of trifles with his sly, dry wit. A cart overturned as a result of the horse bolting: "The horse having a lively imagination and very weak nerves, fancied he either saw or heard something, but has never been able to say what." He found a viper in the garden,

> in close conversation with the old cat, whose curiosity being excited by so novel an experience, inclined her to pat his head repeatedly with her fore-foot; with her claws, however, sheathed, and not in anger, but in the way of philosophical inquiry and examination.

He is forced however to end the interview by beheading the snake with his hoe. He can create a vivid comedy sequence from the little drama where a boy has been convicted of stealing some "ironwork," and sentenced to be whipped at the cart's tail along a stretch of the street. The tender-hearted beadle who was to carry out the punishment, "had filled his left hand with red ochre, through which, after every stroke, he drew the lash of his whip, leaving the appearance of a wound upon the skin, but in reality not hurting him at all." The constable, who followed the beadle, outraged by this clemency, applied his cane to the shoulders of the "too merciful executioner." Thereupon, a young woman, sympathetic to the beadle, slipped in behind the constable, caught the cane, and pulling him back by it, "slapt his face with a most Amazonian fury." In fact, the only person who got off scot free was the thief!

Cowper can even be humorous about the hideous discomforts of their house. The door to the staircase, which opened directly into the only living room, swelled with the damp and refused to open:

> Any attempt to force it upon that office has been attended with such a horrible dissolution of its parts, that we were immediately obliged to introduce a chirurgeon . . . whose applications we have some hope will cure it of a locked jaw and heal its numerous fractures.

In the same way he makes whimsical nonsense of young William Unwin's excuses for delaying a visit because his own house is to be full of workmen:

> As to the masons you expect, bring them with you; bring brick, bring mortar, bring everything that will oppose itself to your journey; all shall be welcome. I have a greenhouse that is too small, come and enlarge it: build me a pinery; repair the garden wall . . . do anything; you cannot do too much.

He was supplied with books by Joseph Hill, who sent the Voyages of Captain Cook, Gray's Letters, and Johnson's *Lives of the Poets*. Cowper appreciated Johnson's good sense and usual sound judgment, but bursts out at his denigration of Milton's *Lycidas:* "Oh! I could thrash his old jacket, till I made his pension jingle in his pocket." But though a volume of his own poems has been accepted by a London publisher, he despairs of producing anything of real value himself:

> Alas, what can I do with my wit? I have not enough to do great things, and these little things are so fugitive, that while a man catches at the subject, he is only filling his hand with smoke.

When Newton was called to a London parish in 1780, Olney seemed emptier than ever, and he wrote to Mrs. Newton that if he was in any condition to leave he would not stay: "I lived in it once, but now I am buried in it, and have no business with the world outside my sepulchre."

What warmed Cowper back to life and provided the stimulus for all his later creative activities was the arrival of a new acquaintance in Olney. She was a Lady Austen, widowed sister of Mrs. Jones, wife of the curate in a neighboring village. At that time she was about forty, not at all good-looking, according to Samuel Greathead, a young clergyman who also often visited Cowper and Mrs. Unwin—though in a sketch of her by Romney she looks ravishing! She was certainly warm and outgoing, however, and Greathead found her the most entertaining person of either sex he had ever met. She had lived much in France with her husband, but had been converted to Evangelicanism after his death, and professed to be seeking a quiet home in the English countryside. Her sister brought her to call on Mrs. Unwin, and she had soon melted Cowper's extreme shyness and charmed them both by her sympathy and vivacity: "She laughs and makes laugh, and keeps up a conversation without seeming to labour at it." It was a long time since Cowper had met anyone from the sophisticated world he had lived in as a young man. He had become a recluse, forcing himself to a monotonous routine of physical activity, reading and writing and rest. Lady Austen upset all that. Within a couple of weeks, we find Cowper writing in jaunty doggerel to Newton, announcing, among other things, a projected picnic. A further letter describes how it lasted most of the day and how he "never made one of a party of pleasure that answered so well." He reports the same to young William Unwin, adding that Lady Austen is "a most agreeable woman, and has fallen in love with your mother and me; insomuch, that I do not know but she may settle at Olney." To Newton, in the following month, he confides that she may repair and renovate the other half of their Orchard Side, and adds: "I am highly pleased with the plan, upon Mrs. Unwin's account, who, since Mrs. Newton's departure, is destitute of all female connexion." He argues in the same tone to William Unwin, noting how Lady Austen's high spirits and readiness of conversation "introduces a sprightliness into such a scene as this . . . which is not the worse for being a little enlivened."

In October Lady Austen returned to London to dispose of her town house, and suggested a correspondence with Cowper. He wrote a verse epistle to their "dear Anna" lauding the wonderful friendship between the three of them, which will prove

> by long fidelity and love
> That Solomon has wisely spoken;
> A threefold cord is not soon broken.

By February, however, Cowper reports to William Unwin that the correspondence has taken a too warm and personal turn; Lady Austen had repeatedly expressed "a sort of romantic idea of our merits, built such expectations of felicity upon our friendship, as we were sure that nothing human could possibly answer." Cowper says he then wrote a cool but tactful response—"Your mother . . . honoured it with her warm approbation"—

> But it gave mortal offence; it received indeed an answer, but such an one as I could by no means reply to, and there ended

(for it was impossible it ever should be renewed) a friendship that bid fair to be lasting.

But he had underrated Mrs. Austen's resilience. Only a few weeks later, Mr. Jones, Lady Austen's brother-in-law, brings "three pairs of worked ruffles" for him, with the promise of a fourth, and in exchange Cowper has sent her his newly published volume of poems. The following month he confesses that further "overtures on her part are to be looked for," and though he and Mrs. Unwin may wish to be more reserved, they must not be rude. In retrospect he sees that the over-hasty intimacy was a mistake. True, Lady Austen had sense and a great gift for talk:

But again he underestimated Mrs. Austen's power to please.

> But her vivacity was sometimes too much for us; occasionally perhaps it might refresh and revive us, but it more frequently exhausted us, neither your mother nor I being in that respect at all a match for her.

By the following July she was back with her sister and came to call. All differences were forgotten: "We are reconciled. She seized the first opportunity to embrace your mother with tears of tenderest affection, and I, of course, am satisfied." Soon he is writing: "We are as happy in Lady Austen, as she in us, as ever." The idea of the joint household was given up, but finally she rented the empty vicarage, and Cowper's "uninterrupted retirement" became "a state of constant engagement." The gate between the gardens was once more in constant use. She liked him to drop in around eleven o'clock in the morning; the two households dined with each other on alternate days; they walked together; she loved the country sights and sounds as much as they did; she listened to his poetry. In the evenings she would play on the harpsichord and sing, or Cowper read aloud while the ladies knitted or sewed. When winter brought the usual depression of spirits to Cowper, Lady Austen's enlivened him. One evening she made him laugh with the story of what happened to a London linen-draper whose plans to celebrate the anniversary of his wedding went awry. Cowper lay awake all night making a ballad of the anecdote. He worked on it with the delighted ladies and sent it off to London, where it was published in *The Public Advertiser* and then as a pamphlet, and soon all London was laughing at *The Diverting History of John Gilpin.* Many editions followed, and several years later Cowper commented: "I little thought, when I mounted him upon my Pegasus, that he would become so famous." Lady Austen also urged him to set about a longer work, and when, as they sat cosily by the fireside, he complained of the lack of subject-matter, she quipped: "Write about anything: write about the Sofa." And so the idea of that domestic epic, *The Task,* was born.

Solomon, however, proved wrong about the strength of a "threefold cord," and the situation became precarious. Samuel Greathead told Hayley, Cowper's first biographer, that Lady Austen's tongue was too sharp and that she "frequently indulged her turn for satire at Mrs. Unwin's expense." Then Cowper was hardly tactful. He presented his Egeria with a lock of his hair, which she had entwined into a brooch. This inspired the verses *To a Lady who wore a lock of his hair set with diamonds,* where the poet is tenderly gallant:

> The heart that beats beneath that breast
> Is William's, well I know;
> A nobler prize and richer far
> Than India could bestow.

We cannot be surprised if Lady Austen believed that Cowper's feelings were stronger than friendship. For her part, she probably thought that she could cure him of his melancholy, detach him from his shuttered and sheltered life at Olney, and make a man of him.

We do not know when Mrs. Unwin reached breaking point, but it seems clear that she did. She had after all given her life

Dorothy Osborne
*by Sir Peter Lely*

Jonathan Swift
*by C. Jervas*

Lady Mary Wortley Montagu
*by Sir Godfrey Kneller*

Horace Walpole,
*a copy of the portrait*
*by J. C. Eccardt*

and her income, and to a certain degree her reputation, to create a safe home for Cowper. She was no doubt glad to have him cheerful and happy, but she was not going to be made to look ridiculous by this younger woman. Moreover she knew Cowper's history and his essential dependence on herself. She must have made it plain to him that the three-cornered situation was impossible and that he must choose his future. We know that Cowper wrote what he described as "a tender and resolute" letter to Lady Austen, making it clear that they must separate. She packed up and left Olney three days later. Cowper wrote to William Unwin a few months later: "Lady Austen is neither returned nor returnable": the episode was closed.

Fortunately new friends created new interests. The Reverend William Bull, schoolmaster in a neighboring village, proved most companionable; "but he smokes tobacco: nothing is perfect." The Throckmortons, a young couple who had succeeded to an estate at Weston, about a mile away, proved most hospitable and generous. They gave Cowper and Mrs. Unwin the freedom of their grounds and gardens at all times. And although Lady Austen had gone forever out of Cowper's life, she had left him a most precious legacy: the stimulus to devote himself to the kind of poetry for which his talents were perfectly fitted. He continued to be haunted by his old demons, "working often in such distress of mind, as, while it spurred me to the work, at the same time threatened to disqualify me from it." But he became absorbed in it, working in the little summer house in the garden, "not much bigger than a sedan chair," surrounded by pinks and roses and honeysuckles; or indoors, in what sounds a very uncomfortable arrangement. He writes to Newton, who disapproves of cards:

> You will wonder when I tell you I write upon a card-table; and will be still more surprised when I add, that we breakfast, dine and sup upon a card-table. In short, it serves all purposes except that for which it was originally designed.

He tells Newton that the poem "has one tendency: to discountenance the modern enthusiasm after a London life, and to recommend moral ease and leisure, as friendly to the cause of piety and virtue." To William Unwin he confides that its particular merit is:

> My descriptions are from nature: not one of them second-handed. My delineations of the heart are from my own experience: not one of them borrowed from books, or in the least degree conjectural.

He chose Unwin to deal with his publisher, and dedicated the poem to him, which offended Newton deeply, as did his refusal to let Newton have a hand in proofreading and revising: "He was fretful and peevish . . . but we shall jumble together again, as people that have an affection for each other at bottom . . . always do."

*The Task* was published in June 1785, and Cowper found himself famous. It was an immediate popular success. Reviewers, clergymen, politicians, all praised it. Hannah More wrote enthusiastically to a friend: "I have found what I have been looking for all my life, a poet whom I can read on a Sunday, and whose *whole* writings I can recommend to my young and my female friends, without restriction or exception." To Cowper, however, the most important aspect of its publication was that it brought some old friends back into his life, particularly his cousin Harriot, Lady Hesketh, now widowed, and living in London with her father and sister. Their close friendship had come to an end after his "conversion," but now she wrote, hoping to see him again. Her letter aroused all the memories of his happy youth in the fifty-four-year-old Cowper and plans for a long visit from her began. Cowper was further stimulated by another literary adventure, a translation of Homer. Although, as a matter of fact, he was most unfitted for the task, he never realized it, and spent six years in the happy delusion that he was eclipsing Pope. But above all, it kept him busy. He knew regular routine occupation was essential for him. As he tells Harriot: "Dejection of spirits, which, I suppose, may have prevented many a man from becoming an author, made me one. . . . Manual occupations do not engage the mind sufficiently. . . . But composition, especially of verse, absorbs it wholly." Moreover, in spite of his infirmity, perhaps indeed because it had so shackled the expression of his talents for so long, his ambition and desire for recognition were now fully awake:

> Till lately, I stole through life without undertaking anything, yet always wishing to distinguish myself. At last I ventured . . . and am determined, if God have not determined otherwise, to work my way through obscurity . . . into notice.

When Harriot arrived finally in June 1786, life was again renewed. She had a carriage, in which they went for drives; they all constantly dined at the Throckmortons—the "Frogs" as they became. Harriot and Mrs. Unwin became fast friends. Everyone enjoyed Harriot, in fact, except Newton, who had never met her. He had already objected to Cowper having anything to do with a pagan author like Homer, and now he wrote to Mrs. Unwin deploring that she and Cowper "have both deviated into forbidden paths and lead a life unbecoming the Gospel." Not only were the Throckmortons Catholics, but to drive for pleasure is worldly, and they have been seen walking on Sunday evenings!

But the days of Newton's influence were over. When Harriot returned to London, she showered them with presents. Someone referred to as "Anonymous" also sent money and gifts. This was Theodora, who had never married, but it does not appear that Cowper ever guessed who the donor was. Finally, after nineteen years in Orchard Side, they moved into a comfortable house at Weston Underwood, that belonged to the Throckmortons: "a house with six sashes in front, two comfortable parlours, a smart staircase, and three bedrooms." Harriot supplied the money for the necessary furniture. Their pleasure in their new quarters, however, was marred two weeks after the move, by the news of the sudden death of William Unwin. Cowper was deeply shocked and grieved and began, in addition to his usual nervous digestive troubles, to have attacks of giddiness and violent headaches: "jarrings that made my skull feel like a broken eggshell." The following winter he was again mentally deranged, but nursed back to rationality in six months by Mary Unwin and Harriot.

For a few years life went on happily enough. His letters are full of belief in his translation of Homer, and the business of getting subscriptions for it. (His publisher finally got five hundred.) He has sound Whig views on politics; is outraged at the "diabolical traffic of the slave trade" and the iniquities of the East India Company, but agrees warmly with Horace Walpole about the take-over of the Company by the Government:

> Were I constituted umpire in this strife . . . I would abandon all territorial interest in a country to which we can have no right, and where we cannot govern with any security to the happiness of the inhabitants.

He welcomes the French Revolution for its ideals of liberty, but regrets the fanaticism of its progress: "They want nothing now but a little English sobriety, and that they want extremely." He feels strongly about the denial of equal rights to Catholics and other dissenters: "To deprive them is persecution; and persecution on any account . . . is an abomination." He exercises with dumb-bells and a skip-rope when the weather is too bad for walking; follows a terrible regime of emetics which is supposed to benefit his stomach, but again, like Horace Walpole, prefers James's Powders to the doctors. His love of animals is as fresh as ever. The hares are all dead, but he gives a lifelike description of the antics of a tortoiseshell kitten. He hopes Harriot will arrive before time, that spoils everything, will turn her into a cat, "for no wisdom that she may gain by experience and reflection hereafter, will compensate the loss of her present hilarity." Or there is the picture of his spaniel Beau, who, having watched him vainly try to reach a water-lily with his cane, plunges into the river, bites the stem, and lays the trophy at his feet.

Cowper delighted in the sense of companionship he found in Harriot, and his letters to her are full of the joy of giving and receiving affection, as well as more practical objects. Exchanges of gifts and commissions for purchases pass to and fro continually, from a cuckoo-clock to a Cheshire cheese. Cowper loved elegance. He delighted in a pair of silver shoe-buckles, he wants some green satin for a waistcoat and a new hat: "Not a round slouch . . . but a smart, well-cocked, fashionable affair." Harriot made him cambric caps, very chic and jaunty, topped by muslin butterfly bows. He asks for silk pocket-handkerchiefs and "a genteelish toothpick case," but was not fortunate with a periwig which Mrs. "Frog" ordered for him:

> My periwig is arrived and is the very perfection of all periwigs, having only one fault; which is that my head will only go into the first part of it, the other half . . . continuing still unoccupied. My artist in this way at Olney has however undertaken to make the whole of it tenantable.

He finds he must refuse a new coat Harriot has suggested for him:

> I thank you for the strip of cloth, commonly called a pattern. At present I have two coats and but one back. If at any time hereafter I should find myself possessed of fewer coats or more backs, it will be of use to me.

In 1790 a young Cambridge undergraduate, John Johnson, a cousin on his mother's side, came to see Cowper, and "Johnny" became almost a son to the poet, paying frequent visits and always bringing good cheer. He is a "wild boy," but his unfailing good spirits, warm affections, and sheer animal vitality delighted the aging Cowper. Homer still occupied working hours and kept up Cowper's hopes of further literary recognition. The translation was published in 1791. No one was very enthusiastic about it, but it led to another proposal from his publisher: an invitation to edit the works of Milton. Cowper was totally unfitted for such a project. While he had an intense love and admiration for Milton, he had no knowledge of editing procedures and no access to a library. Cowper, always incapable of taking decisions for himself, unfortunately chose the worst of advisors. Samuel Teedon, the schoolmaster at Olney, had long admired Cowper, who in earlier days had found him the worst of bores: "the most obsequious, the most formal, the most pedantic of all creatures." Teedon, however, a pious Evangelical, claimed to be a medium for God's messages to man and assured Cowper that the Deity was in favor of the undertaking.

But the Milton project led too to a more stimulating influence. William Hayley, a rich and kindly man though a very bad poet, was at work himself on a life of Milton, and when he heard of Cowper's undertaking, he wrote warmly, suggesting that they consult together. Soon Cowper is calling him "My dear Friend and Brother" and pressing him to come to Weston. He came in May 1792 and a few days later Mrs. Unwin, who had had a slight stroke the year before, had a much more serious one. Hayley's comfort and support helped Cowper through this crisis. He writes to Harriot that Hayley "has made himself so necessary to me in every way in so short a time, that I absolutely know not how to live without him." (Hayley is the only correspondent to whom Cowper speaks of "Mary"; even to Harriot he always calls her "Mrs. Unwin.") But again he went to Teedon for a prognosis, and the schoolmaster could not promise recovery. The fear of losing his beloved friend brought on appalling dreams: "My nocturnal experiences are of the most terrible kind . . . I can hope nothing and believe in nothing."

In the hope of being of help, Hayley urged that he and Mary Unwin should visit him in his Sussex home. Teedon assured Cowper of divine approval and accompanied by

"Johnny" and two servants they made the three day journey by coach. They stayed for six weeks without benefit to either. There was too much company for Cowper's liking. It included, however, the painter Romney, who made a fine sketch of the poet's head, now in the National Portrait Gallery. The face is ruddy, with a long nose and finely cut lips, and large troubled eyes. He is wearing one of Harriot's perky muslin caps.

Things were no better on their return home. Cowper's torturing dreams continued. He took laudanum to give him better nights and he tried to occupy himself with revisions of his Homer, getting up at five o'clock in the morning, as Mrs. Unwin demanded his presence during most of the day. Now unable to feed herself, to read or write or knit, Cowper's sweet and loving companion had changed into an egotistical tyrant. No word of criticism of her ever appears in Cowper's letters, indeed he blames himself for wearing her out, and looks forward with terror to her death. Friends who came to stay, however, were shocked by her demanding possessiveness. When Hayley visited them in November 1793 he reported Cowper as gradually sinking into "hopeless dejection," and the precarious balance in which he had lived so long was never recovered. When Harriot came in January it was difficult to get Cowper to eat or speak: he would sit for hours looking at the ground or pace up and down the room. In May Mrs. Unwin had another stroke. Harriot came to look after the helpless household, but soon it was too much for her health, and since Cowper refused to go to Hayley again, the ever-faithful Johnny, who had an independent income, gave up his curacy to have them live with him in Norfolk.

Cowper went most unwillingly, full of dread. Fragments of a diary written a few days before the move show him in agonizing terrors. "Can any sin . . . deserve what I must suffer?" he asks piteously. Johnny housed them first in the country, then at the seaside, and finally in his rectory at East Dereham, where Mrs. Unwin died a year later. Cowper was so withdrawn into his own misery that he did not seem to feel her loss. The ever-kindly Hayley invented a vision, in which he saw two angelic beings, who proved to be his own and Cowper's mothers, who assured him of Cowper's salvation. Johnny bored a hole between his bedroom and Cowper's, through which he whispered messages from the Deity, promising redemption. Nothing worked. His few painful letters to Harriot tell of his failure to respond any more to natural beauties: a solitary, crumbling pillar of rock standing in the sea seems an emblem of himself: "I stand alone and expect the storm that shall displace me." Worst of all he confesses that he has lost the capacity for affection. The saddest symptom of this change is that the old beloved "Johnny," who was giving up his life to care for him, becomes "Mr. Johnson" in the final letters, and Cowper accompanies this with complaints that his companion tires him with long walks, and upsets him by changes, and is responsible for making him leave Weston.

Just over a year before his death in April 1800, a story he had read years before in Olney came to his mind; a story of a sailor, washed overboard in a storm. His shipmates try to save him; they throw casks and coops and ropes to keep him afloat. Finally, the ship has to sail on, leaving him to drown. In a flash of remembrance Cowper saw the analogy to his own life pattern, and wrote *The Castaway*. His friends had tried to save him, but the ship of life carried them onward, and he, like the sailor, must perish. His doom, though, is spiritual, not physical.

> But I beneath a rougher sea,
> And 'whelmed in deeper gulfs than he.

# Charles Lamb

1775-1834

IN THE LETTERS of Cowper we move in a very different social circle from that of Horace Walpole or Lady Mary, but we are still connected with that world by relatives or friends who belong to it. Cowper himself too, always insisted that on the title pages of his books he should appear as "William Cowper of the Inner Temple Esquire," though he had never had a legal brief in his life, and the title was meaningless. In the letters of Lamb, however, we never touch such circles. We are among the bourgeoisie and the bohemians, men who had to make their livings precariously by their own talents and hard work; who married the daughters of shopkeepers or farmers or poor clergymen; and whose interests are literary or scholarly or politically radical, with never a thought for the socially prominent and powerful.

Charles Lamb himself was, by origin, the poorest of them all. The son of a law-clerk in the Temple, it was only by the influence of his father's employer, Samuel Salt, that he was sent to Christ's Hospital, a charity school, where, however, the standards of education were very high. It was there that Lamb met and made fast friends with S. T. Coleridge, the most brilliant student in the school and destined to go on to Cambridge. Lamb himself, as he described it in a later essay, was "defrauded in his young years of the sweet food of academic institutions." Indeed at the age of sixteen he had to leave school and take a lowly clerkship in the East India House to help support his family. When he wrote his first surviving letter in 1796, when he was twenty-one, Samuel Salt had died, and the family, who had lived in his house (and, for Lamb, had had the wonderful privilege of the freedom of his library), were living unhappily in cramped lodgings. His father was becoming senile, his mother was a querulous invalid, an old aunt quarreled incessantly with his mother, his sister Mary, nine years older than himself, was both nursing her mother and earning money as a dressmaker, and his elder brother John, with a clerkship at the South Sea House, spent as little time as possible at home. Lamb tells Coleridge, to whom all his earliest letters are addressed, that he is "the only correspondent and I might add the only friend I have in the world. I go nowhere and have no acquaintance. Slow of speech, and reserved of manners, no one seeks or cares for my society." He recalls, nostalgically, "the little smoky room at the Salutation and Cat, where we have sat together through the winter nights, beguiling the cares of life with Poesy." He and Coleridge (now married and living at Nether Stowey in Somerset) exchange poems and criticisms, and it is clear that thanks to the teaching at Christ's Hospital and the contents of Salt's library, Lamb is already very widely read in English literature and a most sensitive and penetrating critic of it. It is clear also that, in spite of his loyal devotion, Lamb is very well aware that Coleridge's temperament will cripple his genius. He lets every opportunity of advancement slip. Is it, Lamb asks, "a stubborn, irresistible concurrence of events that causes this, or lies the fault, as I fear it does, in your own mind?"

In September of this year the tragedy occurred which was to affect Lamb's whole life. In a fit of mania, his sister stabbed her mother to death and wounded her father. Charles prevented her being taken to a public asylum and found the money to have her cared for in a private house. Meanwhile he took upon himself the responsibility for the home, his brother being "little disposed (I speak not without tenderness for him) at any time to take care of old age and infirmities." Even as early as this, Lamb showed himself extraordinarily mature in his understanding and sympathies. He was well aware that his mother's rejection of Mary and her open favoritism of her brother John, certainly contributed to her breakdown, and he writes of his own determination: "I am wedded to the fortunes of my sister and my poor old father." He urges Coleridge, who had quarreled with his parents, to foster family feelings: "These are the best foundation for every species of benevolence." At the same time he confesses to the strains of his life, emotional and physical; of evenings when he has had to stay at the office, dinnerless, until seven o'clock, and on his arrival, exhausted, at home, to spend the rest of the evening with his father, at cards or cribbage. Mary soon recovered, but had to be lodged away from home, which again complicated his loyalties and his leisure.

The great event of the following year was a week's visit to Coleridge at Nether Stowey, where Lamb met Southey, Wordsworth and his sister Dorothy, and made final plans for the publication of a volume of poems by himself, Coleridge and Charles Lloyd, a neurotic young man from a wealthy family, whom Coleridge had tutored for a short while. The only notable thing about Lamb's part of the volume was his desire to dedicate it to Mary and his loving reason for doing so:

> It will be unexpected and will give her pleasure . . . [for] there is a monotony of the affections, which people living together, or, as we do now, very frequently seeing each other, are apt to give in to; a sort of indifference in the expression of kindness for each other, which demands that we should sometimes call to our aid the trickery of surprise.

The same thoughtfulness for others, the most endearing trait in Lamb throughout his life, was in a reproof to Coleridge for his lack of sympathetic insight: "You use Lloyd very ill, never writing to him. I tell you again that his is not a mind with which you should play tricks. He deserves more tenderness of you."

The publication of the *Lyrical Ballads* in 1798 delighted him. We have no letters of his on the subject to Wordsworth or Coleridge, but he disagreed with Southey about the merits of *The Ancient Mariner.* He declared he was "totally possessed by it for several days," and that it "plays more tricks with the mind than that last poem, which is yet one of the finest written." This was the famous *Lines written above Tintern Abbey,* which concluded the volume.

In April of the following year Lamb's father died, and he at once moved into lodgings with his "poor dear dearest sister," and began that life of perfect companionship and also of dual loneliness which lasted until his death. Charles was to Mary what Mrs. Unwin was to Cowper, an utterly devoted and dedicated helpmate, but we come far closer to the lives of both of them than we ever do to the intimacies of the household at Olney. They both wrote memorable letters and are both frank and honest to their friends about their difficulties. Though Mary never again had a homicidal attack, she was doomed to a periodic manic-depressive disorder, which recurred almost every year and became longer lasting as she grew older. "What sad, long pieces it cuts out of life," Lamb wrote; and again, in the midst of one of her absences: "Meantime she is dead to me . . . all my strength gone and I am like a fool . . . She is older and wiser and better than me;" and he blames himself when she is well for "teazing her life away . . . with my cursed drinking and ways of going on." Mary, however, writes to Dorothy Wordsworth on one of her returns home:

> I strive against low spirits all I can, but it is a very hard thing to get the better of . . . Charles is very well and very *good* —I mean very sober, but he is very good in every sense of the word . . . I have been a sad trouble to him lately. He has shut out all his friends because he thought company hurt me, and done everything in his power to comfort and amuse me.

Or she writes again:

> It has been sad and heavy times with us lately; when I am pretty well, his low spirits throw me back again; and when he begins to be a little cheerful, then I do the same kind office for him.

The following year, 1806, as she felt she was interfering with his writing, he took a room elsewhere to work in, but after a few weeks of that, she writes to Sarah Stoddart (afterwards Mrs. Hazlitt):

> The lodging is given up . . . and *here he is again*—Charles, I mean . . . as unsettled and undetermined as ever. . . . He could not endure the solitariness . . . I know my dismal faces have been almost as great a drawback upon Charles's comfort, as his feverish, teazing ways have been upon mine. Our love for each other has been the torment of our lives hitherto. I am most seriously intending to bend the whole force of my mind to counteract this.

When they were both well there was no need of any effort to be happy. Mary gives a charming picture of them at work on the *Tales from Shakespeare:* "writing on one table . . . like an old Darby and Joan: I taking snuff, and he groaning all the while and saying he can make nothing of it, which he always says till he has finished and then he finds out he has made something of it." Their fellowship of enjoyment was as complete as their fellowship of depression. The letters are full of glimpses of warm human companionship; expeditions to picture shows, or to the pit at Drury Lane theatre, or wandering round Cambridge colleges; long walks together, visits to friends in the country, parties in their rooms in the Temple or Covent Garden or at the "detached whitish house" at Islington, with its garden, which made Charles feel "like a great lord, never having had a house before." Even in the last year of his life, when Mary was seldom herself, he writes: "When she is not violent, her rambling chat is better to me than the sense and sanity of this world . . . I could be nowhere happier than under the same roof with her."

All Charles' friends loved Mary, recognizing her as a remarkable woman, full of humor, wisdom, and sympathy. Charles said: "Of all the people I ever saw in the world my poor sister is the most thoroughly devoid of the least tincture of selfishness." It would have cut her to the heart to know that her presence in the household prevented a happy marriage between Charles and their young actress friend, Fanny Kelly, to whom he proposed in 1819, when he was forty-four. He wrote to congratulate her on her latest success at Drury Lane, but he knew she did not really enjoy her profession and longed to give it up:

> I am not so foolish as not to know that I am a most unworthy match . . . but you have for years been a principal object in my mind. In many a sweet assumed character I have learned to love you, but simply as F. M. Kelly I love you better than them all. Can you quit these shadows of existence and come and be a reality to us?

Miss Kelly wrote in reply that while she was "not insensible to the high honour which the preference of such a mind as yours confers upon me," that nevertheless "an early and deeply rooted attachment" had fixed her heart elsewhere. To her sister, however, she wrote the truth:

> I was indeed sorry to refuse him, for he shows the most tender and loyal affections . . . [But] I could not give assent to a proposal which would bring me into that atmosphere of sad mental uncertainty which surrounds his domestic life.

Yet the first twenty-five years of the century held much more pleasure than pain for the Lambs, in spite of their early extreme poverty, in spite of Mary's attacks and Charles' "cursed drinking and ways of going on." As to Lamb's drunkenness, it can easily be exaggerated. As early as 1801 we find him apologizing affectionately to a friend for nearly upsetting a boat at a picnic and for some frivolous remarks about religion: "You know that a very little liquor will cause a considerable alteration in me." There are three later humorous and repentant letters to other friends for "passing out" at their parties and having to be carried home and put to bed—luckily Lamb was very small and light! Until the last years of his life, however, when he drank to escape his loneliness and his heartache over Mary, his drinking was simply social. Unfortunately he wrote a fictional essay, *Confessions of a Drunkard,* and never managed to live down the story that it was a true account of his own excesses. In general, along with his smoking, which he was always vowing to give up, it was part of his delight in congenial and warm good-fellowship, and it is as the perfect companion that we picture Lamb most clearly.

Hazlitt and others have given accounts of the famous Thursday evenings at the Lambs, with "cards and cold mutton, gin and jokes." The host with his small, fragile frame and "almost immaterial legs," surmounted by his fine head, black curly hair, bright brown eyes and expressive features: "After first seeing him, you did not think any more of his ridiculous body." The hostess, that "incomparable old maid," dispensing the meat and the "heaps of smoking roast potatoes," in a setting of worn old furniture, Hogarth prints and crowded bookshelves. "How we cut into the haunch of letters: how we picked out the marrow of authors!" said Hazlitt, and Lamb's stammer did not interfere with the brilliance of his talk. Wordsworth, in a memorial poem, spoke of his

> Humour and wild instinctive wit, and all
> The vivid flashes of his spoken words.

He came, however, to find his reputation as good company somewhat of a burden to him. He writes "joco-seriously," to Mrs. Wordsworth, in 1818, of the impossibility of ever being alone:

> Except my morning's walk to the office, which is like treading on sands of gold for that reason, I am never so . . . I could

> sit and gravely cast up sums in great books . . . and yet reserve in some corner of my mind . . . faint memory of some passage in a book, or the tone of an absent friend's voice, or a gleam of Fanny Kelly's divine plain face. But there are a set of amateurs of the Belles Lettres, who come to me as a sort of rendezvous, putting questions of criticism. . . . Their noise ended, one of them accompanies me home, lest I should be solitary for a moment: he at length takes his welcome leave at my door; up I go, hungry as a hunter, hope to forget my cares in the agreeable abstraction of mastication; knock at the door, and in comes Hazlitt or Mr. Martin Burney, or my brother, or somebody, to prevent my eating alone, a process absolutely necessary to my wretched digestion . . . I am saturated with human faces . . . I am never C.L. but always C.L. and Co.

In spite of this he found time to write, though all his early work was uniformly unsuccessful. His poems went unnoticed; his novel, *Rosamund Gray,* dropped still-born from the press; his poetic tragedy, *John Woodville* was refused by the management of Drury Lane, his farce, *Mr. H.,* on which he built great hopes, was hissed off the stage on the opening night. *The Tales from Shakespeare* and some children's stories, written with Mary, brought in a little money, as did the *Specimens of English Dramatic Poets contemporary with Shakespeare, with Notes.* This last was the fruit of his enormous reading in the byways of literature, and introduced the public to many of the Elizabethan playwrights who had been completely forgotten. His Notes were full of felicitous criticism, and illustrated again his unerring literary taste. Just as his critical conversation delighted his friends, so his letters are full of discoveries from writers of the past and comments on those of the present. He championed Blake, both as draughtsman and poet, when almost no one knew of his existence. Like Keats, he discovered Chapman's Homer and contrasts it favorably with Cowper's translation: "Cowper's damned blank verse detains you every step with some heavy Miltonism; Chapman gallops off with you at his own free pace." Lamb immediately recognized the genius of Wordsworth and was a warm friend of the whole family all his life, but he finds Wordsworth's streak of vanity and pomposity at times almost more than he can stomach. To his friend Thomas Manning, safely in China, where he will not pass along any scathing remarks, Lamb feels he can be frank in his criticism. He describes how Wordsworth had sent him a copy of the second *Lyrical Ballads* in 1800, at the same time apologizing for not acknowledging or criticizing Lamb's play *John Woodville* (which he had sent many months before), because of an "almost insurmountable aversion from letter writing." Lamb acknowledged the poems, characteristically picking out the best things in the volume, the Lucy poems, for special notice, but praising it all. He added, however, one small criticism about the danger of direct didacticism.

> The Post did not sleep a moment. I received almost instantaneously a long letter of four sweating pages from my Reluctant Letter-Writer, the purport of which was that he was sorry his second volume had not given me more pleasure . . . and was compelled to wish that my range of sensibility was more extended.

A few years later, to Manning again, he reports that Wordsworth has come to London: "He says he does not see much difficulty in writing like Shakespeare, if he had a mind to try it. It is clear then nothing is wanting but the mind." Nevertheless he loved and respected Wordsworth too, though he never made any secret of the fact that he thought Coleridge the greater genius, though a ruined one. To Wordsworth himself Lamb writes in 1816 that he has seen Coleridge at the home of the Highgate apothecary, Mr. Gillman, "where he plays at leaving off laudanum." Even so,

> his face, when he repeats his verses hath its ancient glory, an Archangel a little damaged . . . the neighbourhood of such a man is as exciting as the presence of fifty ordinary persons. 'Tis enough to be within the whiff and wind of his genius, for us not to possess our souls in quiet.

He is at home among all the minor literary figures of the age; Southey, Rogers, Hazlitt, de Quincey, Godwin, Leigh Hunt, Thomas Hood, and wrote an enthusiastic review of Keats' last volume, finding St. Agnes' Eve "next to Wordsworth in excellence." The only individual he really hated was "that damned infernal bitch," the second Mrs. Godwin, with her ill-bred manners and her interference with her husband's friendships. She was the mother of Clare Clairmont, later the mistress of Byron and mother of his daughter Allegra. Of all the literary figures of his day, Byron is the only one for whom Lamb has nothing good to say: "I have a thorough aversion to his character and a very moderate admiration of his genius—he is great in so little a way."

When Lamb was a young man of twenty-one and in the stage of complete infatuation with Coleridge, Coleridge wrote a poem in which he addressed his friend as "gentlehearted Charles." Some years later, when the poem was reprinted, the more mature Lamb burst out: "For God's sake, don't make me ridiculous any more by terming me gentle-hearted in print, or do it in better verses." He points out that the epithet suggests mawkishness. Coleridge certainly did not intend such an interpretation, and probably wanted to praise the warmth of heart and the sweetness of nature which all who knew Lamb felt as the essence of his charm. Landor wrote a poem on his death, saying that he left

> The love of friends without a single foe:
> Unequalled lot below.

He had friends among extraordinarily different people, both men and women, and valued each as a distinct individuality. As he wrote to Wordsworth in 1822:

> Two or three have died within the last twelve-month, and so many parts of me have been numbed. One sees a picture, reads an anecdote, starts a casual fancy, and thinks to tell it

> to this person in preference to every other: the person is gone whom it would have particularly suited. It won't do for another. . . . Thus one distributes oneself about; and now for so many parts of me I have lost the market. Good people, as they are called, won't serve. I want individuals. I am made up of queer points and I want so many answering needles.

It is impossible to read the letters without feeling the generous presence of a man who was ever ready to consider others before himself and was full of unselfconscious selflessness. His first published letter tells Coleridge that he has paid a bill for him and that any repayment would be "superfluous"; his last letter is one of anxiety lest he should have lost a friend's book. He showed endless wry patience over his impossible friend George Dyer, with his "sublime belief in the immortality of his own writings and his utter ignorance that the world doesn't care a pin about them." A characteristic episode took place when the Lambs had just moved into new rooms in the Temple. Dyer "scrambled up to the door about breakfast time," dirty and unshaven, announced he was dying and that Charles must take charge of all his unpublished manuscripts, which he had brought with him. He then lay down on Charles' bed and sent for "his little dirty niece" and a still dirtier little nephew, to bid them farewell. The Lambs suspected that his chief complaint was lack of food, and sure enough, a good meal revived him. Charles ends the story resignedly: "I shall not be sorry when he takes his nipt carcass out of my bed, and vanishes with all his lyric lumber." But for years he never did vanish for very long, and was obviously one of those queer fish who are much more amusing to read about than to have around.

Lamb saw no reason himself why possessors of the creative temperament should not pay their debts, support their families and avoid petty squabbles; but though he did all these things, he was forever helping the failures and the unfortunates. We find him continually trying to raise money or get jobs for Coleridge or Godwin or Leigh Hunt and other impecunious hangers-on. He buys paper for Hazlitt to print what he himself regards as "an imprudent political pamphlet," and undertakes endless practical commissions for the muzzy-minded Coleridge. He earned Leigh Hunt's lifelong gratitude for his regular visits when Hunt was imprisoned for a libel on the Prince Regent. All the quarrels between Wordsworth and Coleridge, between Coleridge and his "pensive Sara," between Hazlitt and *his* Sarah—and with almost everyone else—between Leigh Hunt and Godwin, left Lamb friendly with all sides. At Hazlitt's death, since his family had all deserted him, Lamb made all arrangements for the funeral and was one of the only two mourners at it. He spent hours of precious leisure reading and commenting kindly on a translation of Homer by the old father of a friend, or on Godwin's dreary poetic tragedies, or Southey's epics or the verbose and lifeless poems of Bernard Barton. Lamb indeed, who was not a churchgoer had, as one friend said, "more of the essentials of Christianity in him than ninety-nine per cent of professing Christians."

His friends loved him for his unfailing loyalty and unselfishness, but they must also have loved him for his capacity for playing the fool and pouring out witty nonsense. Cowper had a delightful playful humor in describing the daily doings of his uneventful life, but Lamb has a vitality of personality Cowper lacked, and it communicates itself in his raillery and absurdity as much as in his moods of seriousness. He often apologizes for the untidiness of his communications: "I am the worst folder-up of a letter in the world, tho' I hear there is a peasant in Moldavia who does not know how to fold one up at all." But his correspondents must have found that easy to forgive when the letter was opened. He wrote wonderful sustained comic descriptions, too long to quote, of a visit to a well-known bluestocking, of the horrors of moving house or of convalescing by the sea on a wet Sunday. But his humor is everywhere. It may be just an aside: "I always spell plumb-pudding with a b . . . I think it reads fatter and more suetty"; or a horrified warning to Manning in China not to get among the obviously cannibal Man-chews: "Tis terrible . . . to sit at table not as a guest, but as a meat." He is filled with equal horror at the time of the Burke and Hare trials for body snatching, when he hears that a young friend has married a chemist: "Pray heaven he may not have done it for the sake of trying chymical experiments upon her—young female subjects are so scarce." He knows what Landor is suffering on a visit to the country:

> I forgot to tell you, I knew all your Welsh annoyances, the measureless Beethams—I knew a quarter of a mile of them—17 brothers and 16 sisters as they appear to me in memory. There was one of them that used to fix his long legs on my fender, and tell a story of a shark, every night, endless, immortal. How have I grudged the salt-water ravener not having had his gorge of him!

When a friend has taken charge of Lamb's dog, Dash, he writes to enquire about his mental health.

> Are his intellects sound, or does he wander a little in his conversation? You cannot be too careful to watch the first symptoms of incoherence. Try him with hot water. If he won't lick it up, it is a sign he does not like it. . . . Is his deportment cheerful? I mean when he is pleased—for otherwise there is no judging. . . . Has he bit any of the children yet? If he has, have them shot, and keep *him* for curiosity, to see if it was the hydrophobia . . .

He can profess equal concern about himself, as he answers the letter of a woman friend who is nursing a houseful of children with the measles. He declares that suddenly he is feeling far from well:

> You did not let any of the children touch the seal with their little measly hands, did you? . . . I look at your note—I see it is wafered, not sealed. That makes it more likely—Wafers are flour, and I've known a serious illness to be communicated in a piece of plum-cake . . .

He gives a lifelike description of all the physical and mental symptoms of a bad cold, ending: "I am flatter than a denial or a pancake . . . I acknowledge life at all, only by an occasional convulsive cough. . . . My hand writes, not I, from habit, as chickens run about a little when their heads are off." Then he adds innocently:

> Yet do I try all I can to cure it, I try wine and spirits and smoking and snuff in unsparing quantities, but they only seem to make me worse . . . I sleep in a damp room, but it does me no good; I come home late o'nights, but do not find any visible amendment.

Bernard Barton, the completely humorless Quaker poet, to whom this was written, evidently replied in great distress at Lamb's plight and Lamb has to tell him that he took it "in too serious a light." In another letter he cannot resist chaffing Barton with much solemnity. A forger had just been hanged and Lamb sends a long, straightfaced letter imploring B.B. not to start stealing from the Bank where he is employed, but to stand firm against temptation. Let him remember how it would reflect on his faith: "thousands would go to see a Quaker hanged"—and also what a bad effect it would have on the sale of his poems.

Barton suggests in one of his early letters that he might give up his clerkship in the bank and try to live by his pen, and Lamb is not joking when he replies vigorously to *that* idea:

> Throw yourself on the world without a rational plan of support, beyond what the chance employ of Booksellers would afford you!!! Throw yourself rather, my dear Sir, from the steep Tarpeian rock, slapdash headlong upon iron spikes.

Lamb, who had the constant examples of Coleridge, Godwin, Hazlitt, Leigh Hunt and other friends all trying to make a living by free-lance writing, knew, only too well, its dangers and miseries. He points out the blessing of a steady job: "What, is there not from six to eleven p.m. six days in the week, and is there not all Sunday?" And as to the disadvantages of a sedentary life: "Think of the patience of tailors—think how long the Chancellor sits—think of the Brooding Hen."

As Lamb grew older, however, he hated more and more the drudgery of his deadening routine in the "candle-lit fog-den" in the City. Constantly he had to put in overtime in the evenings, which provoked the explosion: "Confusion blast all mercantile transactions . . . and rot the very firs of the forest that look so romantic alive and die into desks." In 1818 he reports angrily that the East India House "have abridged us of the immemoriably observed custom of going out at one o'clock of a Saturday, the little shadow of holiday left us," and adds with biting irony that probably the Committee has arranged a scale of permissions for leave of absence, ranging from four days a year after fifty years' service, to one day after eighteen years', "but not without leave of the Chief." In the following year he wrote a letter to Coleridge in red ink, which he calls "Clerk's Blood," and again bursts out: "Damn 'em! my brains, guts, skin, flesh, bone, carcass, soul, TIME, is all theirs." In 1822 he puts his position to Wordsworth:

> My theory is to enjoy life, but the practice is against it. I grow ominously tired of official confinement. Thirty years have I served the Philistines. . . . You don't know how wearisome it is to breathe the air of four pent walls without relief day after day, all the golden hours of the day . . . O for a few years between the grave and the desk! . . . I dare not whisper to myself a Pension on this side of absolute incapacitation and infirmity, till years have sucked me dry . . . I sit like Philomel all day (but not singing) with my breast against this thorn of a desk, with the only hope that some Pulmonary affliction may relieve me.

The *Elia* essays, which made Lamb's name as a writer, had started in "The London Magazine" in August 1820. In the following year he tells Dorothy Wordsworth: "How I like to be liked, and *what I do* to be liked! They flatter me in magazines, newspapers and all the minor reviews." Probably his new fame had something to do with the decision of the East India House to grant him a pension in 1825, after thirty-three years' service. He did not develop any pulmonary affliction, but his request for retirement was supported by medical evidence that his health required it. At the age of fifty, therefore, he found himself free, with a pension of two-thirds of his salary. He wrote to Wordsworth:

> I came home for ever on Tuesday. . . . The incomprehensibleness of my condition overwhelmed me. It was like passing from life into eternity. . . . I wandered about thinking I was happy, but feeling I was not. But that tumultuousness is passing off. I am daily steadying, and shall soon find it as natural to me to be my own master, as it has been irksome to have had a master.

But he never found it natural. As so often, longed-for retirement brought its own frustrations. At first he spent long hours reading the Garrick collection of plays in the British Museum, "a treasure rich and inexhaustible—2000 of them." But after a few months he tells Coleridge he is in a "nervous fever" from the amount of sociability he has to take part in:

> Never any poor fellow was so befriended as I. Do you know any poor solitary human that wants that cordial to life—a true friend? I can spare him twenty, he shall have 'em good cheap. I have gallipots of 'em—genuine balm of cares . . .

To escape too much company, and as they thought, to benefit their health, they moved in 1827 to Enfield, ten miles outside London. But it proved disastrous. It was too far away for busy friends to visit frequently, and though no doubt Lamb had hoped that he would fill his time with his own writing, his creative zest was exhausted; he wrote nothing but some poor poems. "Infirmities and fretfulness grow upon us," he wrote. Mary's attacks became more frequent and prolonged, and now it was loneliness and lack of friends that oppressed Charles. His only amusement was to go for long walks, "but deadly long are the days—these summer all-day days, with but a half-hour's candlelight and no firelight." He is writing here to Barton, whom he had advised earlier to stick to his job, and he concludes: "I pity you for over-work, but I assure you no-work is worse. The mind preys on itself, the most unwholesome food. I brag'd formerly that I could not have too much time. I have a surfeit." He signs himself "Yours forlorn."

To Mary Shelley (the poet's widow) he describes the horrors of the village:

> Clowns stand about what was once the Market place and spit minute-ly to relieve ennui. . . . We have for indoor amusement a Library without books, and the middle of the week hopes of a Sunday newspaper to link us by filmy associations to the world we are dead to.

The world they were dead to was London, and London had been Lamb's life-blood. As a young man he had confessed to Wordsworth that he was not "romance-bit about Nature," and that he found the city much more stimulating.

> Separate from the pleasure of your company, I don't much care if I never see a mountain in my life. . . . The lighted shops of the Strand and Fleet Street, the innumerable trades, tradesmen and customers, coaches, waggons, playhouses; all the bustle and wickedness round Covent Garden; the very women of the town; the watchmen, drunken scenes, rattles; life awake, if you awake, at all hours of the night . . . the crowds, the very dirt and mud, the sun shining upon houses and pavements, the print shops, the old book-stalls, coffee houses, steams of soups from kitchens, the pantomime—London itself a pantomime and masquerade—all these things work together in my mind, and feed me, without a power of satiating me . . . I often shed tears in the motley Strand from fulness of joy at so much life.

Later, when in 1817, they moved from the quiet of the Temple to rooms where they see Drury Lane Theatre out of their front windows and Covent Garden from the back, they are both ecstatic about the situation. Mary writes to Dorothy Wordsworth: "the hubbub of the carriages returning from the play does not annoy me in the least—strange that it does not, for it is quite tremendous"; and Charles adds: "We are in the individual spot I like best in all this great city."

To combine his retirement from the regular routine of his office with a removal from this life-long familiar environment, could not fail to produce profound nervous or emotional miseries. In 1830 he tells Wordsworth that he has sunk into "respectable insignificance" and must be content:

> Yet in the self-condemned obliviousness, in the stagnation, some molesting yearnings of life, not quite killed, rise, prompting me that there was a London, and that I was of that old Jerusalem. In dreams I am in Fleet Market, but I wake and cry to sleep again . . . O let no native Londoner imagine that health, and rest, and innocent occupation . . . can make the country anything better than altogether odious and detestable.

Later that year, when Mary was ill, he did try living in London lodgings for a while, but found he could no longer take the pace of his old convivial life among his friends. Finally, since Mary was so often incapacitated, and so that she should not be "fluttered with continual removals," he arranged that he should join her at the home of a Mr. and Mrs. Walden, at Edmonton, where she had been cared for several times before. The Waldens agreed to have no other patients. From there, in 1833, Lamb wrote again to Wordsworth, adding "prayers for dear Dorothy," who had also lost her mind:

> Mary is ill again. Her illnesses encroach yearly. . . . In short half her life is dead to me, and the other half is made anxious with fears and lookings forward to the next shock. . . . I see little of her: alas! I too often hear her. *Sunt lachrymae rerum!* and you and I must bear it.

A year later Coleridge died, and his friends said that the thought of it never seemed to leave Lamb. He would interrupt himself and them to say suddenly: "Coleridge is dead." A few months later, in December 1834, when Mary was again sick, he set out one morning for "The Bell" public house, stumbled over a stone, fell, and cut his face. No one thought he was badly hurt, but the wound became infected with erysipelas and he died five days later, at the age of fifty-nine. Mary lived for another twelve years, until she was eighty-two.

# George Gordon, Lord Byron

1788-1824

AFTER BYRON'S death at Missolonghi, Edward Trelawney found an unfinished canto of *Don Juan* among his papers. It contained the following verse:

> Temperate I am—yet never had a temper;
> Modest I am—yet with some slight assurance;
> Changeable too—yet somehow *'Idem semper'*:
> Patient—but not enamoured of endurance;
> Cheerful—but, sometimes, rather apt to whimper:
> Mild—but at times a sort of 'Hercules furens':
> So that I almost think that the same skin
> For one without—has two or three within.

Byron also started a novel, which did not get very far, but gave this description of the hero:

> It was evident that he was a prey to some cureless disquiet; but whether it arose from ambition, love, remorse, grief . . . or merely from a morbid temperament akin to disease, I could not discover . . .

Byron, in fact, though his life and loves have been the material for comment and interpretation for nearly a hundred and fifty years, still remains enigmatic: the same skin held so many opposing qualities. Most obvious is the legendary Byron built up from the heroes of his earlier poetry; from his own social rank, magnetic personality, and physical beauty, and from the scandals surrounding his life in London from 1812 to 1816, culminating in the separation from his wife. Eight years later this figure became a national hero who gave his life in the cause of Greek independence. The figure is a dramatic, indeed a melodramatic, one: demonic and sadistic at times, a fiery adventurer, a sensuous voluptuary, a faithless though passionate lover, arrogant yet tender, but with it all a lonely spirit, cynical and melancholy, filled with "some cureless disquiet."

Much of this was a true picture. Byron believed fervently in heredity, and on both sides of his family he came from ancestors of whom plenty were violent, lawless, and dissolute. His father, "Mad Jack Byron," had to leave the country to escape his creditors. He died when Byron was three years old, and the child was brought up by a coarse-grained, undisciplined mother and a Calvinistic nurse, who seems to have combined impregnating his mind with ideas of predestination and initiating him into erotic realities before he was ten years old. Unexpectedly, at that age, he inherited his title from his great-uncle, known as "the Wicked Lord." Byron told his lifelong friend John Cam Hobhouse how he remembered the deference of the headmaster of his school as he told him the news. He was called into the study and given cake and wine, and this little treat and the master's respectful manner at once gave him "high notions of his new dignity." He never lost them. He was reckless and spendthrift and took advantage of his rank and property to incur enormous debts. In Venice he lived in a palace with a retinue of sixteen liveried servants and kept eight horses, four carriage and four saddle, several carriages, and a yacht. At the same time he was writing his banker friend, Douglas Kinnaird, who looked after his financial affairs, not to trouble to pay the debts he owed tradespeople before he left England. He was moody, restless, vain and egocentric; he had a streak of heartless cruelty and a savage temper; he loved to dramatize himself. His love affairs were legion. He was always "in a scrape" of some sort in the way of an amorous intrigue, or of several at once. Yet he claimed that he had never seduced a woman and there seems no reason to doubt his word. Once when a friend remonstrated with him about a new "affair," Byron quipped: "I have been more ravished myself than anybody since the Trojan War." His fatal sexual attractiveness made women compete wildly for his attention. His own amorous feelings were easily aroused and he enjoyed the pursuit, but once caught, he tired quickly of his conquests, discarded his loves without pity and was then snatched up by new ones. He combined a complete slavery to women with a complete contempt for them. Only Teresa Guiccioli finally managed to hold his affections and loyalty for any length of time, and even then he chafed: "It is awful work, this love, and prevents all a man's projects of good and glory."

He did have a vision of good and glory, and indeed everything in Byron which repels one is matched by qualities and behavior which are powerfully attractive. All his emotional instability melts away in his relations with his men friends. Hobhouse said "his power of attaching those about him to his person was such as no one I ever knew possessed." He shows his forthright good sense in replying to a cool letter from Tom Moore, whom he supposed he had offended: "So, if I have,—why the devil don't you say it at once, and expectorate your spleen?" His affectations are balanced by his sincerity, his arrogance by his humility, his irrational impulses by an essential sanity. He can show a basic honesty about his weaknesses, which is very endearing, and a generosity and sense of justice which outweighs them. His warmth of sympathy toward friends and dependents was unbounded and he could be the best of company, full of robust good humor, wit and laughter.

This "doubleness" of nature, with its bewildering paradoxes of mean and noble attributes runs all through his correspondence. His egotism, his rebel nature, and his ambition are all alive in his schooldays. A letter from Harrow when he was fifteen declares that he has been accused unjustly of a fault, and announces flatly: "If I am treated in this manner, I will not stay at this school." To his half-sister Augusta, six years his senior,

William Cowper
*by George Romney*

Charles Lamb
*by William Hazlitt*

Lord Byron
*by G. W. Harlow*

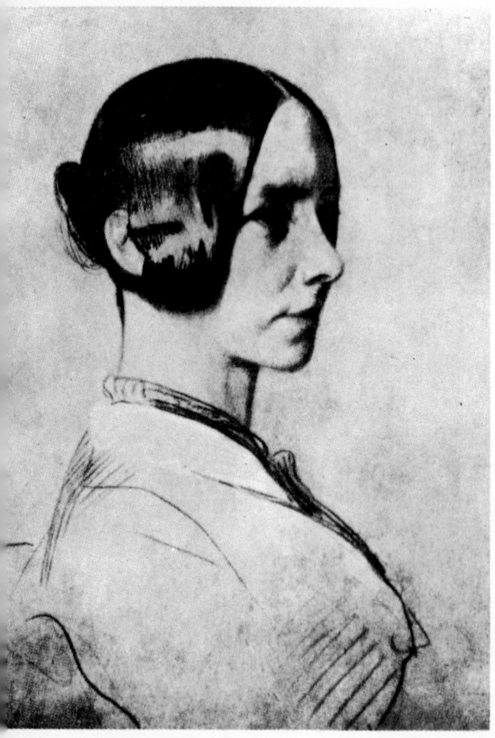

Jane Carlyle
*by Samuel Lawrence*

Edward FitzGerald

he confides, in the following year, his hatred of his mother, "whose *diabolical* disposition . . . seems to increase with age, and to acquire new force with Time." Yet it is to his mother, in the same year, that he confides his sense of his own potentialities:

> The way to *riches,* to *greatness* lies before me. I can, I will cut myself a path through the world or perish in the attempt.

He was happy enough at school and his lameness did not prevent his playing in the cricket team against Eton, and in swimming, always his favorite exercise. Though intensely self-conscious about this disability, which required him to wear a specially built boot and padded calf on his right leg, and gave him a kind of "sliding gait," it seems to have interfered very little with any of his activities.

He went to Trinity College, Cambridge, in 1805, where his career was not distinguished. "My life has become one continuous routine of dissipation," he confesses to his lawyer, "Wine and women have *dished* your humble servant, not a *sou* to be had." When he left three years later he retired to the dilapidated family estate, Newstead Abbey, in Nottinghamshire, until he came of age in January 1809. Then he announced his intention to travel and set out, with Hobhouse as a companion, and his devoted valet, Fletcher, who never left him afterwards. His half-sister had married her cousin, Colonel Leigh, "that very helpless gentleman," who lived for race-meetings and had as many debts as Byron himself. He wrote a farewell letter to Augusta, delighting in the prospect of escaping from his mother:

> I can never forgive that woman . . . for I think I had naturally not a bad heart; but it has been so bent, twisted and trampled upon, that it has now become as hard as a Highlander's heel-piece.

His mother was an unsympathetic character, but we may suspect that she too had a good deal to put up with. Byron had moods of affection for her and he wrote to her regularly on his travels. These lasted until the summer of 1811, and included Portugal, Spain, Malta, Albania, Greece and Turkey. His letters are guide-book stuff and not interesting. Summoned home by a stoppage of funds and demands for his presence by his lawyer, he is full of good intentions:

> I mean to cut all my dissolute acquaintance, leave off wine and carnal company, and betake myself to politics and decorum.

On his way through London, he gave a long manuscript poem he had written on his travels to an admiring distant relative, Robert Dallas, with permission to do what he liked with it.

Just as he was preparing to leave for Newstead, word came that his mother had had a stroke, and before he arrived she was dead. Byron was deeply shocked and he spent some months at home, correcting the proofs of his poem, which Dallas had placed with John Murray for publication. He dramatized himself in a Byronic pose:

> At twenty-three I am left alone, and what more can we be at seventy? It is true I am young enough to begin again, but with whom can I retrace the laughing part of life?

However he is more fun in an invitation to Augusta to come for a visit with her family:

> I don't know what Scrope Davies meant by telling you I liked children. I abominate the sight of them so much that I have always had the greatest respect for the character of Herod. But as my house is large enough for us all, we should go on very well.

He plans to drive her from Newmarket in his carriage and "we can have a cage for the children and a cart for the nurse. Or perhaps we can forward them by canal."

At the end of October he moved to London, made great friends with Tom Moore, the popular Irish poet, and found his publisher, Murray, to be a very intelligent and agreeable person. He lived quietly, went to theaters, heard Coleridge lecture, and worked on his poem. In February 1812 he made his maiden speech in the House of Lords. The Nottingham hosiers had introduced machines which took the place of six handworkers. Riots broke out among the workless and they wrecked some of the frames. Troops were sent in. A bill was introduced by the Government to make the rebels liable to the death penalty. Byron wrote to Lord Holland of his intention to speak on the subject:

> However much we may rejoice in any improvements in the arts which may be beneficial to mankind, we must not allow mankind to be sacrificed to improvements in mechanism . . . I have seen the state of these miserable men, and it is a disgrace to a civilized country. . . . Their grievances call rather for pity than punishment.

The speech delighted the Whigs, and Holland House, the great social center of politics, was open to Byron. But this new political distinction was eclipsed two weeks later, when Murray published the first two cantos of *Childe Harold's Pilgrimage.* "I awoke one morning and found myself famous," Byron wrote, and his world became transformed. He had created a new cult. Not only was the hero of his poem a romantic adventurer, a passionate lover, a cynical yet melancholy and haunting figure, but the reality of the poet himself proved to be equally fascinating: a nobleman of an ancient family; young, handsome, with curly auburn hair and long-lashed gray-blue eyes, beautifully cut features and a pale delicate skin. His manner was "Byronic," aloof and slightly disdainful, but that made him even more attractive to women. Byron kept a great number of letters from his admirers of all classes, and such of these as have been published suggest that the allegedly prudish young women of the early nineteenth century were indeed no different from those of the present day in their unabashed expressions of love for a popular idol.

The most infatuated and uninhibited of them all was Lady

Caroline Lamb, who wrote in her journal after their first meeting: "That beautiful pale face is my fate." As a matter of fact Byron himself was really more attracted to Lady Melbourne, Caro's mother-in-law. He had a strong craving for maternal love, which he had never had in any understanding way, and Lady Melbourne supplied this. At the same time she was highly intelligent and, as Byron said of her later, "excited an interest in my feelings that few young women have been able to awaken." He tells her in one letter that she is "the supreme woman," whom he loves better than any being on earth. His letters to her during the next few years are the most revealing he ever wrote. To her, he has no secrets, and it is through this correspondence that we watch the progress of his affair with Caro—and with others.

The "little volcano" was undoubtedly fascinating, but full of egotistical vanity, headstrong and impulsive, and with a sublime lack of consideration for anything but her own caprices. Her young husband (later the famous Lord Melbourne of Queen Victoria's reign), was quiet, indolent, and indulgent. She was infatuated with Byron, and it was his first experience of a relationship with a woman of his own rank. He was flattered and charmed by her provocative personality. But he had not bargained for her complete lack of discretion and her possessive jealousy. Her behavior became an open scandal. She demanded his company at all hours and would burst into his rooms uninvited. Byron remonstrated:

> I never knew a woman with greater or more pleasing talents. But these are unfortunately coupled with a total lack of common conduct.

In fact she was making Byron ridiculous by her escapades. He continued to write love letters and verses to her, but it was with the greatest relief that he heard that her mother, Lady Bessborough, was taking her to Ireland in September. He wrote to Lady Melbourne: "You will not regret to hear I wish this to end, and it certainly shall not be renewed on my part."

A few days later, to impress her with his determination, he confesses to Lady Melbourne that he is seriously attached to another young woman, with the idea of marriage:

> One of whom I never said much, but have never lost sight of . . . The woman I mean is Miss Milbanke. . . . I know little of her, and have not the most distant reason to suppose that I am at all a favorite in that quarter. But I never saw a woman whom I *esteemed* so much.

It was Lady Caroline who had introduced her cousin Annabella Milbanke to Byron and had sent him some of her poems. At that time, however, he had declared that though "she certainly is a very extraordinary girl . . . I have no desire to be better acquainted. . . . She is too good for a fallen spirit to know, and I should like her better if she were less perfect." Lady Melbourne now offered to sound out her niece's feelings by reporting Byron's sentiments towards her. This she did, and Miss Milbanke refused the proposal. Byron thanked Lady Melbourne for her "efforts with my Princess of Parallelograms" (Miss Milbanke was interested in mathematics), but he did not take his disappointment very hard. A month later he writes to Lady Melbourne:

> I cannot exist without some object of love. I have found one with whom I am perfectly satisfied, and who as far as I can judge is no less so with me; our mutual wish is *quiet*, and for this reason, I find a double pleasure (after the ridiculous display of last season) in repose.

His beloved was Lady Oxford, a beautiful and intelligent woman of forty, well known for her infidelities to an unattractive husband, but serene and undemanding. Byron took a house near her country estate in Herefordshire and passed a peaceful winter, writing his poem *The Giaour*. His peace, however, was punctuated by wild letters from Caro, pleading for a reconciliation, and when he came to London in the spring, she continued to plague him with her histrionics, culminating in her trying to cut her wrists at a ball at which they were both present. *The Giaour* proved another huge success, but meanwhile the affair with Lady Oxford had cooled and she had gone abroad in June. Late in the same month Augusta, whose feckless husband was as usual absent at some race-meeting, decided to escape her clamorous creditors and children by coming on a visit to London. Byron had seen little of her since his return from abroad, but he had always been devoted to her. She, like the much older Lady Melbourne, understood him instinctively, and he was completely at his ease with her. She was loving and lovable, as well as beautiful and always full of gaiety and simple, uncomplicated warmth: the very antithesis of Caro. By August Byron is writing to Tom Moore:

> I am at this moment in a far more serious and entirely new scrape than any of the last twelve months—and that is saying a great deal. (It is unlucky we can neither live with or without these women.)

What happened that summer was to have fatal consequences for Byron. That his relationship with Augusta was incestuous there seems no doubt, but that it was his deepest experience of love is equally certain. It contained all the contradictory elements in his own nature: the simple craving for shared tenderness, the love of bravado and the sense of something demonic and dangerous in his passion. He confessed later to Lady Melbourne that there was "a mixture of the terrible" in his feeling which made other relations "uninteresting and insipid." Guss, or Goose, as Byron used to call her, for her wits were not her strong point, was, we can guess, basically amoral; she speaks of her "iron nerves and elephant constitution." She loved to give pleasure and to make others happy; she loved her young half-brother, and she had a faithless husband and a difficult, debt-ridden domestic life. The visit to London must have seemed a fairy story. She took the parts of sister, friend, lover as if they were all quite natural. Certainly she had none of the restless, guilt-ridden moods which afflicted Byron, who seems to have combined a secret pride in breaking the moral law, with an occasional profound sense of sin about it. Yet he wrote to Guss later that the experience left him "utterly incapable of real love for any other human being—for what could they be to me after *you?*" He confided to Lady Melbourne a plan for going abroad with Guss, and that shocked even that extremely sophisticated woman of the world. She replied: "You are on the brink of a precipice, and if you do not retreat, you are lost for ever." Byron replied that her arguments were "unanswerable" and that they had had the effect she wished. Augusta left London in August, though they were together again for three weeks at Newstead in the winter. A daughter was born to her the following April and in announcing it to Lady Melbourne, Byron seems to accept his paternity. He adds:

> You must however allow that it is utterly impossible I can be half so well liked elsewhere, and I have been all my life trying to make someone love me, and never got the sort that I preferred before.

His secret was safe with Lady Melbourne, but with almost inconceivable folly, and disloyalty to Augusta, Byron seems to have betrayed the situation by innuendoes elsewhere; worst of all, to Caro. She declared that when she paid a last visit to his rooms in 1814, "he showed me letters, and told me things I can't repeat." She was to repeat them later with dire results.

But that was in the future, though already, before Augusta had left London, Annabella Milbanke, after a formal meeting at a party, had written Byron a long letter professing friendship and admiration, and urging him to have an object in life! Before that disastrous relationship was seriously established, however, another of Byron's "scrapes" intervened, and as he reports it, play by play, to Lady Melbourne, it reads more like scenes from a Restoration comedy than anything else. In September a Cambridge acquaintance, James Webster, invited him to stay at his country house in Kent. Byron reports that his hostess, Lady Frances, seems a very good, well-disposed girl, but "she evidently expects to be attacked, and seems prepared for a brilliant defence; my character as a roué has gone before me." The husband, jealous, but himself promiscuous, amuses Byron by openly preaching a double standard of sexual morality in marriage. Meanwhile he and Lady Frances exchange opening shots, as it were, over a game of billiards. As usual with Byron, it is she who takes the initiative by posing a hypothetical question: What should a woman do, if she liked a man and he did not realize it? Byron responded with a short note, hidden by the lady in her bosom just as her husband comes in. An answer is slipped to him with "a little too much about virtue, and indulgence of attachment in some sort of ethereal process, in which the soul is principally concerned . . . but as my proselyte is only twenty, there is time enough to materialize." A postscript to this letter to Lady Melbourne, added the same evening, says there has been a passionate scene in which she evidently threw herself into his arms: "her expressions astonished me, so young and cold as she appeared." Luckily no one came in, but he ends: "we must be more cautious."

The next letter describes a scene in which the husband congratulates himself "on possessing a partner without passion." Byron adds: "I cannot yet speak with certainty, but I never yet saw more decisive preliminary symptoms," though he has to confess sadly, "the topography of this house is not the most favorable." More notes pass, and he gives her a lock of his hair, commenting apologetically: "She is so young a beginner that you won't wonder at these exchanges and mummeries." Yet ten days later he is confessing he is "totally absorbed in this passion," and goes on madly: "I am even ready to take a *flight* if necessary, and as she says, 'We cannot part,' it is no impossible dénoument." The next day, he is in hopes it may develop into a temporary "affaire reglée," but if not they will probably elope. Several days later, when they have all moved to Newstead, his hopes collapse. Left alone together, she has almost yielded: "I give myself up to you"—but fear of subsequent feelings of guilt and remorse terrify her. "Was I wrong? I spared her," says the frustrated Don Juan. He feels a fool, and yet "she seems so thankful for my forbearance." Meanwhile, the husband is suspicious, the sister is suspicious, "we are all as wretched as possible . . . I can foresee nothing—it may end in nothing. . . . What a cursed situation I have thrust myself into!"

Luckily, it did end in nothing. Byron left for London, and by the end of November he hints to Tom Moore of a recent escapade in the country, and adds: "However, 'Richard's himself again,'" and that he doesn't think very much about it now. It was just another illustration of Byron's extraordinary capacity to fascinate women, and of his own incapacity to resist any amatory adventure that presented itself. On Lady Frances' persistence in writing impassioned letters and his own cold responses, he comments wryly to Lady Melbourne: "If people will stop at the first tense of the verb 'aimer,' they must not be surprised if one finishes the conjugation with someone else." He turned to writing, as he always did as an escape from living, and finished his second Turkish Tale. He notes in his Journal: "It was written to drive my thoughts from the recollection of—'Dear sacred name, rest ever unreveal'd'"—(who was certainly not Lady Frances). The poem was *The Bride of Abydos,* the story of a boy and girl who believe themselves to be brother and sister, and love, and die.

Byron took up his usual London life again: gay stag parties, orgies of over-eating and drinking, followed by bouts of fasting on dry biscuits and soda water, refusals of literary parties at the Misses Berry's or at Madame de Stael's, attendance at fashionable dinners at Holland House, visits to the opera and the theatre, fencing and boxing bouts. And, as usual, efforts to dodge Caro. She kept forcing her way past the faithful Fletcher, into his rooms. "I can't throw her out of the window," Byron complains, but she has "no shame, no feeling. . . . If there is one human being whom I do utterly *detest* and *abhor* it is she." Meanwhile a regular correspondence has been established with Miss Milbanke. In January 1814 he writes to Lady Melbourne:

> I do believe that to marry would be my wisest step—but whom? . . . all wives would be much the same. I have no *heart* to spare and expect none in return. . . . What I want is a companion—a friend rather than a sentimentalist. I have seen enough of love matches.

At around the same time he notes in his Journal the arrival of a letter from Annabella, and comments in very favorable terms on her personality:

> She is a very superior woman, and very little spoiled, which is strange in an heiress—an only child . . . who has always had her own way. She is a poetess—a mathematician . . . and yet withal very kind, generous and gentle.

She had told him that her parents knew of their letters but asked him to tell no one else. Needless to say he told Lady Melbourne of the situation: how Annabella, strictest of virgins, a moralist and religionist, had started the correspondence, "with a personage generally assumed to be a great roué," which seemed a strange contradiction. In April, he declares he is not in love with her, but "I do admire her as a very superior woman, a little encumbered with Virtue." He also notes "a dependence upon her own infallibility which will or may lead her into some egregious blunder." He cannot make up his mind whether to accept an invitation to stay with her parents at Seaham, near Durham: "I have no judgment and less common sense than an infant."

This is only too true. He is at the mercy of his moods and impulses. In the same month he writes in his Journal:

> I do not know that I am happiest when alone; but this I am sure of, that I never am long in the society even of her I love . . . without a yearning for the company of my lamp and my utterly confused and tumbled over library.

He has spent four days in his rooms, exercising by boxing for an hour in the mornings:

> The more violent the fatigue, the better my spirits for the rest of the day; and then my evenings have that calm nothingness of languor, which I most delight in.

He knows that he is wasting his life, "daily repenting and never amending"; he knows that a Parliamentary career is open to him; "but I have no ambitions . . . past events have unnerved me; and all I can now do is to make life an amusement." He is too indolent and egotistical to examine himself honestly, and drifts along, unstable, confused, undisciplined, and falls back on fatalism: "I have always believed that all things depended upon Fortune and nothing upon ourselves."

He evaded the invitation to Seaham, writing tartly to Lady Melbourne: "If she imagines that I . . . delight in canvassing the creed of St. Athanasius, or prattling of rhyme, I think she will be mistaken." In June he was relented and the letters grow warmer. By August he has written the fatal words: "I did—do—and always shall love you." But Annabella played "hard to get," and wondered if he could make her happy. Byron could play that game too, and replied: "Very well—now we can talk of something else." She asked for a list of books on modern history, and Byron softened again: "Are the 'objections' to which you alluded insuperable? or is there line or change of conduct which could remove them?" Annabella capitulated: "If I can make you happy, I have no other consideration. I will trust to you for all I should look up to—all I can love." To Lady Melbourne Byron wrote: "I mean to reform most thoroughly. . . . Seriously, I will endeavour to make your niece happy." Annabella, he says, is to be not only his love, "but my first friend, my adviser, my reprover when necessary." Moore thought her "too straitlaced" for Byron, but Augusta, always affectionate and optimistic, was full of enthusiasm. The first visit to Seaham in November was not, however, very successful. He took an instant dislike to his future mother-in-law, and after ten days wrote that Annabella's disposition was not what he had thought it. Back in London, he found himself involved in money difficulties. The sale of Newstead, through which he had hoped to pay his heavy debts and have an assured income, had fallen through. He thought it might be better to postpone the wedding, but to this Annabella would not consent. As he traveled north with Hobhouse, who was to be best man, Hobhouse recorded: "Never was lover less in haste." They arrived several days after they were expected, but Hobhouse noted that Annabella seemed "dotingly fond" of Byron. They were married very quietly in the drawing room at Seaham on January 2, 1815.

In everything that happened, or that Annabella alleged to have happened, during the disastrous year of marriage, we have to remember that all her evidence was written after the separation, at the prompting of her legal advisors, and for the express purpose of convicting Byron. No doubt he behaved extremely badly; he never denied it, but he had unfortunately married a woman who had two fatal flaws: she had no sense of humor, and she had an unshakeable self-complacency about her own rectitude. She had attracted Byron because, unlike all other women, she had not at once succumbed to his charm, which piqued his vanity. But it was largely her own lack of warmth and spontaneity which had armed her in the beginning, and she had finally made a calculating campaign to marry him, in the firm belief that she could reform him into her own conventional pattern. Her love was to tame this wild erratic creature into a docile domestic animal. No calculation could have been more mistaken. The only women who could ever hold Byron were those who could laugh with and at him. Augusta and Teresa Guiccioli were gay and easy, knew when to leave him alone, knew when he was teasing and when he was serious, and could melt his histrionics into humanity by tenderness or raillery.

According to Annabella's later account, Byron's behavior was psychopathic from the wedding day onward. While Byron was writing in his usual affectionate tone to Lady Melbourne, telling her that Bell was lying "fast asleep on a corner of the sopha," and "you would think we had been married these fifty years," she was to report that his manner was frenzied, his temper malignant, that he hinted at dark sins in his past, kept pistols by his bed and threatened her with violence. On their way south they stayed with Augusta. To Augusta, the past was past. She loved Byron devotedly, but now he was a marrried man and she welcomed her sister-in-law with all her usual warmth. According to Annabella later, Byron behaved abominably, sending her up to bed while he stayed to talk with their hostess. Yet soon after they reached London, Annabella wrote asking if Augusta will remain a sister to her and Augusta replied:

> You will ever be my own dearest Sis . . . *Indeed, indeed,* every day makes you if possible dearer . . . I can't say half enough, you know I'm always dumb when I feel most, and *you* understand that.

As soon as they arrived in London, however, Byron was overwhelmed with money problems. Lady Melbourne had foolishly rented a large, expensive house for them. Newstead was unsold, a Lancashire estate Byron owned was tied up in litigation. Annabella had proved not to be much of an heiress after all. The rumor that she was had brought all his creditors down on him at once. Within the next nine months bailiffs were in the house ten times. Byron, at his wits' end for funds, and plagued with nervous indigestion, must have been extremely difficult to live with. He had bouts of heavy drinking, and as he said of himself, "wine and spirits make me sullen and savage to ferocity." Annabella was pregnant, and Byron had fits of affectionate solicitude for her, though at other times he was "cold and sneering," with "a love of tormenting." However, when on a visit to Newmarket, his letters to her begin, "Dearest Pip," and are signed "Ever most lovingly thine," while Annabella calls him "Darling Duck." He gives a comic description of the disorder of the household and that "Goose is taking a quill from her wing to scribble to you—so—yours always most conjugally."

Annabella had begged Augusta to be with her for her confinement, and she was an immense comfort to her sister-in-law, as Augusta always had a calming effect on Byron's extravagances. She too, however, was perturbed by his behavior. He continued to drink and keep late nights with his men friends, insisted on having his meals alone, and "abandoned himself to every sort of desperation" about his finances. The baby girl was born in December, and since bailiffs were in the house and it had to be given up, it was agreed that Annabella and the child should go to Seaham as soon as she could travel.

They set out on January 15. Annabella posted an affectionate letter from her first stopping place, and on her arrival sent another to "Dearest Duck" and ending:

> If I were not always looking about for B., I should be a good deal better already for country air . . . Love to the good Goose, and everybody's love to you both from hence.
>
> Ever thy most loving Pippin.

This letter was difficult to explain afterwards, but Annabella declared that, believing her husband to be insane, she had thought it best to humor him! She had indeed consulted doctors about him and had asked her own physician to see him as soon as she left, and report on his condition. The doctor did this promptly, and assured her that Byron, though bad-tempered and violent, was sane.

Annabella seems then to have taken an immediate decision

to leave him, and for the first time, told her parents of her marital problems. Her mother rushed up to London for legal advice and on February 2nd her father wrote a stiff letter to Byron asking him to appoint a legal representative to discuss the terms of separation. To Byron this was a complete bombshell: he was stunned and incredulous. Thoroughly accustomed as he was to live his life by the dictates of his own impulses, he seems to have taken it for granted that his wife would tolerate his excesses and accommodate herself to his alternations of charm and egotistical perversity. He wrote a dignified reply, declaring that it was not true that he and his wife had parted in anger, that his financial crisis, intensified by bad health had made him moody and irritable, but that he would take no steps about a separation without his wife's sanction. At the same time he wrote to his "Dearest Bell" begging her to consider what was at stake: "My errors, or by whatever harsher name you choose to call them, you know; but I loved you and will not part from you without your express and expressed refusal to return to or receive me. Only say the word that you are still mine in your heart."

Annabella's reply was unequivocal. She declared she had seriously and dispassionately reviewed the misery she had experienced from the day of her marriage, and had determined on a separation. Byron was pathetically puzzled and hurt in his reply:

> I still cling to the wreck of my hopes, before they sink forever. Were you then never happy with me? . . . Have no marks of affection of the warmest and most reciprocal attachment passed between us? or did in fact hardly a day go down without some such? . . . I have not denied my state of mind —but you know its causes—and were these deviations from calmness never followed by acknowledgment and repentance?

On February 15, he sent another appeal:

> I know not what to say, every step taken appears to bear you further from me. . . . Of the charges to be preferred against

> me I have *twice* been refused any information by your father and his advisors . . .
>
> I have invited you to return; it has been refused. I have requested to know with what I am charged; it is refused. Is this mercy or justice? . . . And now Bell, dearest Bell, whatever may be the event of this calamitous difference . . . I can only say that I love you, bad or good, mad or rational, miserable or content, I love you, and shall do, to the dregs of my memory and existence.

But Annabella had decided that she had acted "from the strictest principles of Duty," and that "Feelings must not now be indulged." On February 22 she came to London and gave her lawyer a detailed written account of all her suspicions about the earlier relations of Byron and Augusta. But that was for legal eyes and ears alone, in the event that the case came into court, and Byron claimed custody of his daughter. By the standards of the age, drunkenness, infidelity, and violence were not sufficient grounds for Annabella to claim a legal separation and to keep the child. The gossip which soon became widespread arose most likely from Byron's own earlier indiscretions, and particularly from Lady Caroline Lamb. Byron's friends prevailed on Annabella to sign a written denial that she was the source of the rumors, but Byron always believed her to be. Lady Melbourne held aloof. She had always feared such disclosures, and she sent a message requesting Byron to destroy her letters to him. Augusta herself, all unaware of Byron's treacherous indiscretions, simply denied everything. She was, however, torn with conflicting loyalities. She pleaded with Annabella to give Byron another chance. Annabella herself realized Augusta's goodness of heart, and though her lawyers refused to let her see her, she wrote to her mother:

> She has been the truest of friends to me . . . and I hope you regard her, and *seem* to regard her as such, for I very much fear that she may be supposed the cause of the separation by many, and it would be cruel injustice.

It was not the matter of Augusta—for Annabella knew very well that marriage had ended that—it was not the influence of her mother, though Byron always believed it to be—it was simply Annabella's rigid and implacable nature that determined the separation. She mistook obstinacy for dignity, and her decision once taken as Duty was upheld at every turn by chilling self-justification and moral self-complacency. She declared that she had "escaped from the greatest villain that ever existed," and that he had tried to make a joke of it. Byron had indeed tried complete simplicity: "Dearest Pip, I wish you would make it up—for I'm dreadfully sick of all this, and cannot foresee that any good can come of it." Finally, though, on March 4, he prayed her with deep sincerity not to sacrifice her own happiness as well as his: "Oh Bell, to see you thus stifling and destroying all feeling, all affection, all duties (for they are your first duties—those of wife and mother) is far more bitter than any possible consequence to me."

His friends urged him to fight the case in the courts, but he refused—no doubt for Augusta's sake—and consented in the middle of March to a private settlement. He made no answer to the scandalous attacks and accepted full responsibility himself. In a letter to Moore immediately afterwards he insists that Annabella was an "amiable and agreeable" wife:

> The fault was *not* . . . in my "choice" (unless in *choosing at all*)—Where there is blame, it belongs to myself, and if I cannot redeem, I must bear it.

He makes her family the external villains, and gives his own health, his "strange and desultory bachelor habits" and his money troubles as causes (but not excuses) for his excesses. Finally he owns that his pride recoils from the *indignities* of it all: "However, I have no quarrel with that same pride, which will, I think, buckler me through everything."

It did; though not without moods of self-pity, in one of

which he wrote, and published, the poem, "Fare thee well! and if for ever/Still for ever, fare *thee well*"; and other moods of fury against the "moral Clytemnestra" who had deserted him, blasted his name, and robbed him of his child. In a final note to Annabella he begs her to be kind to Augusta: "For never has she acted or spoken towards you but as your friend." On April 26, 1816 he left England, never to return.

From Geneva, where he spent some months he wrote to Augusta that he was in good health, "but for all that she—or rather the separation—has broken my heart, I feel as if an elephant had trodden on it." At the same time he has to confess that "a foolish girl, in spite of all I could say or do, would come after me, or rather went before—for I found her here. I did all I could to prevent it, and have at last put an end to it." This was Clare Clairmont, daughter of that second Mrs. Godwin whom Lamb found so intolerable. Clare had forced herself upon Byron during the miserable months of social ostracism, and had now come to stay with her half-sister Mary Godwin, and Mary's lover, the poet Shelley, and to announce that she was pregnant. Byron had not "put an end to it" and its sequel was to show him at his very worst. He and Shelley, however, became very good friends, and he worked hard at Canto III of *Childe Harold*. He said later that he was half mad at the time of its composition, and should many times have blown his brains out "but for the recollection that it would have given pleasure to my mother-in-law." As for his deepest feelings, he tells Augusta: "I shall never find anyone like you—nor you (vain as it may seem) like me. We are just formed to pass our lives together."

In November he reached Venice, where he was to spend the next three years. In 1817 Newstead was at last sold, and Byron lived lavishly, with a large menagerie of pet animals, soon joined by his small daughter Allegra, whom he refused to leave with Clare. He passed his time "viciously but agreeably," working busily on *Don Juan* and on his *Memoirs,* which, when completed in 1819, he put into the hands of Moore for publication after his death. He wrote frequently and with great freedom to Augusta:

> We may have been very wrong—but I repent of nothing except that cursed marriage—and your refusing to continue to love me as you had loved me. I can neither forget nor *quite forgive* you that precious piece of reformation.

Yet the humiliation of the separation is never far from his mind. Two years later he is still saying: "It has completely swallowed up in me every other feeling," and he still persuades himself that a reconciliation is possible. He had no men friends in Venice, just a succession of Italian mistresses. He writes to his banker friend Douglas Kinnaird that he meant to give up "gallivanting" on leaving England, but as his health returned the need to love "came back upon my heart again, and after all, there is nothing like it." Shelley, who visited him in 1818 reports: "He says he disapproves . . . he is heartily and deeply discontented with himself." However he continued to pass from one "scrape" to another, until in April 1819 he met Teresa Guiccioli, nineteen years old, married to a rich landowner of sixty, who had already had two wives and families. The Countess was gay, elegant, voluptuous, and intelligent; rather short and plump, but with red-gold hair and animated features: "as fair as sunrise and as warm as noon," Byron tells Augusta. To Teresa he wrote: "You should not have re-awakened my heart . . . for my love has been fatal to those I love —and to myself. But these reflections come too late—I am, and eternally shall be, entirely yours." Some months later his tone has shifted and he confides to Augusta: "I feel—and I feel it bitterly—that a man should not consume his life at the side and on the bosom of a woman, and a stranger . . . and this Cicisbean existence is to be condemned." Yet he cannot break free: "to leave or to be left would at present drive me quite out of my senses." To Hobhouse he says he thinks seriously of taking Allegra and going to South America: "Better be an unskilful planter . . . than fan-carrier to a woman. I might still be a decent citizen. I could at all events occupy myself rationally." Obviously he was feeling a bitter sense of homelessness and exile from his own environment. His only escape was in his poetry and he worked continuously at that.

Count Guiccioli had at first appeared a complaisant husband and willing to accept Byron as his wife's *cavaliere servante,* but in 1820, when he had followed the Countess to Ravenna, the adultery became too open and the Count insisted on a legal separation. The Papal Court ruled that she was to live with her father Count Gamba, and Byron wrote: "I am, of course, in an awkward situation enough." The following year Count Gamba, who had taken part in the rebellion against Papal and Austrian political domination, was banished from Ravenna, and moved to Pisa. Byron and his retinue of course followed. Pisa was near Leghorn, where Shelley and Mary (now his wife) lived, and Clare Clairmont frequently stayed. Byron was determined to keep Allegra from her mother and the Shelleys, though they had cared for Clare at the time of the child's birth and for fifteen months afterwards. Now he declared that he would not have her starved on a vegetarian diet, "or be taught to believe there is no Deity," and he insisted on leaving her in a convent near Ravenna. We cannot be too sympathetic to Clare and what Byron rightly described as her previous "Bedlam behaviour," but Byron's behavior now was most brutal. He paid no attention to Clare's letters pleading to see her child, and he never went to see her himself. Clare sent a friend to report on the conditions in the convent, and he brought back accounts of its damp situation and poor food. Both Clare and Shelley then begged Byron to remove Allegra, but he was quite pitiless. Clare wanted to try an abduction, but Shelley wrote to her that though it tore his heart to think of their helplessness, "Lord Byron is inflexible and he has her in his power." In April of the following year Allegra died of typhoid fever; she was just over five years old.

Byron had been becoming more and more frustrated and restless at his Epicurean life: "One must face an object of attainment, not to rust in the scabbard altogether." He was in sympathy with all revolutionary movements, and he foresaw that "the king-times are fast finishing" and that "the people will conquer in the end." He had been bitterly disappointed at the failure of the Italian revolt and was following closely the situation in Greece. He longed to be active, "but the tears of a woman who has left her husband for a man, and the weakness of one's own heart are paramount." However, when Byron received a letter from the Greek Committee in London asking his support, he took a final stand.

> If I left a woman for another woman, She might have cause to complain, but really when a man merely wishes to go on a great duty, for a good cause, this selfishness . . . is rather too much.

He wrote offering his services to the Committee and asking to be sent to the Levant to seek information at first hand. On July 16, 1823 the disastrous expedition set out. It met frustrating obstacles at every turn, and Byron's exasperation reflects itself in his Journal: "I did not come here to join a faction, but a nation, and to deal with honest men and not with speculators and peculators." Rival parties were incriminating one another in their struggle to get hold of the funds Byron controlled: "the worst of them is that they are such damned liars." He had to spend the rest of the year at Cephalonia, trying to mediate between the factions. At the end of January 1824 he reached Missolonghi, a small fishing town surrounded by swampy marshland. It rained incessantly. Byron found his British colleagues inefficient and all plans to attack the Turks came to nothing. Yet he never regretted having taken the decision to act, and found a deep interest in trying to impose a sense of responsibility and organization on his motley followers. But before anything could be accomplished, in April he was stricken with fever, treated by incompetent and frightened doctors, and bled and purged to death in an atmosphere of squalid confusion. He was thirty-six.

In 1819 Byron had written to Murray that after his death,

> I hope they won't think of pickling me and bringing me home . . . I am sure my bones would not rest in an English grave, or my clay mix with the earth of that country. I believe the thought would drive me mad on my deathbed.

But that was just what was done. Byron was now a hero, and his friends hoped he would be buried in the Poet's Corner in Westminster Abbey. The Dean and Chapter refused, and his body was taken to the little church of Hucknell Torkard, the village near Newstead, where his ancestors were buried.

But even before that the Byron controversy had broken out afresh. Moore had the *Memoirs.* Byron had told him that he had "omitted all the really *consequential* and *important* parts" of his early life and loves, "except in a general way," and many other things which might compromise others:

> But you will find a detailed account of my marriage and its consequences, as true as a party concerned can make such accounts, for I suppose we are all prejudiced.

The news of Byron's death reached England on May 14, 1824. On May 17, six men, only two of whom had even read the *Memoirs,* met in Murray's house in Albemarle Street. One was sensible enough to suggest putting the manuscript in a safe until it could be studied carefully, and if necessary, left for posterity to judge. Moore protested that there was very little scandalous material at all, but panic prevailed, and the entire manuscript was solemnly burnt in the fireplace. So Byron himself was silenced, while many who had had only the slightest connection with him rushed into print to turn their reminiscences, however slight or slanted, into cash. The controversies around him have lasted ever since, and he remains a battle-ground.

He was completely clearsighted about the value of his own poetry, and had no vanity about his easy fame. It is another strange paradox that a man whose ideal poet was Pope should have written Byron's romantic gush. But poetry was his escape. "It is a relief from the fever of my mind to *write*" he says, and again: "All convulsions end with me in rhyme." Writing was "a way of getting rid of thinking." It came in wild bursts of energy, but he had no power of sustained discipline. His own literary taste—compared, for example, with that of Lamb—was very poor. He rated Campbell and Rogers, who have now sunk without trace, in the first rank of contemporary poets. He knew, however, that satire was his own true element and *Don Juan* his masterpiece. Murray was timid about its publication, and wanted cuts, but Byron refused to have the poem gelded: "It shall be an entire horse or none"; and to Kinnaird he wrote:

> As to *Don Juan*, confess, confess—you dog and be candid—that it is the sublime of *that there* sort of writing—it may be bawdy, but is it not good English? It may be profligate, but is it not *life*, is it not the *thing*?

This is the real Byron speaking, not that histrionic mask of the misanthropic romantic adventurer that his public loved. And this is the voice we hear in the letters; they are full of his own energy and vitality and a reflection of his innumerable moods. Full of self-dramatization, of course, since that was innate in him, but full too of spontaneity and masculine vigor. While we can sympathize with Annabella on the morning after one of his uproarious stag-parties, on October 15, 1815, his description of it to Moore sounds as if a good time was had by all:

> Like other parties of the kind, it was first silent, then talky, then argumentative, then disputatious, then unintelligible, then altogethery, then inarticulate and then drunk . . . and to crown all, Kinnaird and I had to conduct Sheridan down a

> damned corkscrew staircase, which had certainly been constructed before the discovery of fermented liquors, and to which no legs, however crooked, could possibly accommodate themselves.

The talk, he says, was very good, but the wine carried away his memory, "So all was hiccup and happiness for the last hour or so, and I am not impregnated with any of the conversation."

He was always generous and willing to help anyone in distress. He wrote to Moore from Venice in 1816:

> I hear the Edinburgh Review has cut up Coleridge's *Christabel* and declared against me for praising it. I praised it, firstly, because I thought well of it; secondly, because Coleridge was in great distress, and after doing what little I could for him in essentials, I thought the public avowal of my good opinion might help him further.

(We feel that had Lamb known of this, he would have forgiven Byron anything.) He can be equally outspoken about his enmities. He helped Leigh Hunt because of his liberal principles, not because he liked the man, and when the Hunts took over Shelley's house after Shelley was drowned in July 1822 he is outspoken to Mary. She must send back a sofa he had given her husband, he writes: "I have a particular dislike of anything of Shelley's being within the same walls as Mrs. Hunt's children. They are dirtier and more mischievous than Yahoos." Byron, in fact, preferred Lady Frances Webster's household: "The place is very well and quiet, and the children only scream in a low voice." He liked his creature comforts and no one has suggested better the horrors of a formal English dinner-party in winter:

> Why does Lady Holland always have that damned screen between the whole room and the fire? I was simply petrified. All the rest, too, looked as if they were just unpacked, like salmon from an ice-basket.

Yet with all its wit and good spirits and good-nature, and in spite of the poetry that has survived, it was a wasted life. Byron himself told Moore in 1818 that he did not regard poetry as his real vocation, but that if he lived for ten years he would make his name in a different sphere. He meant as the leader of some liberal cause, and all his deepest instincts came from that. Had he not been too lazy and too woman-ridden to continue a political career in England, he might have made his name in some really substantial way. He had the brains and intelligence for it, as well as the courage and independence. In Europe, though it was the overthrow of monarchical tyranny and the servitude of poverty that, as was natural, seemed to him the immediate objects of liberalism, no one has been so prophetic as he about the dangers of future tyrannical dictators. Writing in 1822, he quotes a remark that literature "is the great engine by which all civilized states must ultimately be supported or overthrown." He adds that he thinks it is difficult to decide whether the most potent "engine" in the hands of a government is literature, or religion, or education. He concludes:

> It is certain, however, if by any means it could obtain all three, its influence would be unbounded, and a nation so enslaved would enjoy only an automaton existence, following every impulse of its rulers.

All too little of this Byron appears in the letters, or anywhere else; it was "the buried life" that could never get free. Yet though we have seen plenty of evidence of Byron's fatal flaws —his vanity, his egotism, his poses, his violence, his capacity for real cruelty—plenty remains on the other side. Hobhouse and other friends, having failed to get permission for his burial in Westminster Abbey, asked that the fine bust by Thorwaldsen might have a place in Poets' Corner. The request was refused, and the bust is in the Library of Trinity College, Cambridge, but part of Hobhouse's petition might stand as Byron's epitaph:

> Lord Byron had failings—many failings, certainly, but he was untainted by any of the baser vices; and his virtues . . .

> were all of the highest order. He was honorable and open in all his dealings and he was kind. . . . He was true-spoken—he was affectionate.
>
> Lord Byron was totally free from envy and jealousy. . . . He was well aware of his own great reputation; but he was neither vainglorious nor overbearing. . . . Indeed he was, in the best sense of the word, a gentleman.

It may give us some small satisfaction that his daughter Ada, Countess of Lovelace, who died before her mother, requested in her will that she be buried beside her father.

# Jane Carlyle

1801-1866

JANE WELSH wrote to her lover Thomas Carlyle in the spring of 1824: "If they had said the sun and the moon was gone out of the heavens, it could not have struck me with the idea of a more awful and dreary blank in the creation than the words: Byron is dead." It gives some idea of the impression that Byron made on his contemporaries that this daughter of bourgeois Scottish Presbyterian parents should have made him her idol, but she had not then outgrown her romantic youth, which did not last very long.

She was then twenty-three, living with her widowed mother in the small town of Haddington, in the south of Scotland, which she described to a friend in Edinburgh as "at the bottom of the pit of dulness . . . it is the dimmest, deadest spot (I verily believe) in the Creator's universe." She and her mother had little in common. Her father, a doctor, who died when she was eighteen, had been her intellectual stimulus, and encouraged her in her reading and in independence of mind. Her mother's only interests were in housekeeping, paying calls, giving tea-parties in her drawing-room, full of "a superfluity of elegant whimwhams," and in trying to find a suitable husband for Jane. This last was the only interest they shared. Jane was attractive to men, and her early letters are full of a series of flirtations without much emotional content.

Nor did the early meetings with Carlyle provoke much. We

hear of him first in a letter urging her Edinburgh friend to read Rousseau's *La Nouvelle Héloïse*. She fears she will never meet anyone like the hero St. Preux; but she continues:

> I have just had a letter from Thomas Carlyle. He is something like St. Preux. . . . He has his talents, his vast and cultivated mind, his vivid imagination, his independence of soul and his high-souled principles of honour. But then—ah, these Buts! St. Preux never kicked the fireirons, nor made puddings in his teacup. . . . Want of elegance, Rousseau says, is a defect which no woman can overlook.

This was probably written in July 1821, and the original meeting had been in May. Carlyle was then twenty-five, doing literary hackwork in Edinburgh, full of discontent and loneliness, tortured physically by constant nervous indigestion, and spiritually by the consciousness of powers within himself still undiscovered and faculties unexercised. His peasant parents had dreamed of him in the ministry, but that had no appeal to him. He tried schoolmastering, but found that "teaching school is but another name for sure and not very slow destruction"; the law proved no better: "a shapeless mass of absurdity and chicane." He felt his prospects to be "a shadowy void," his best days "hurrying darkly and uselessly away." Yet he had an inner certainty that if he could find "a way of authorship" suited to his own voice, he could "make the doors of human society fly open before me."

Carlyle fell in love with Jane at first sight. His first letter is written a few days after his return to Edinburgh from a visit to a school friend in Haddington. He sends books and says he may bring more shortly, for "Positively I must see you soon, or I shall get in a very absurd state." He closes with the familiar symptoms that he feels as if he had known her for twenty years and that "I somehow think you *understand* me." For the moment, however, Jane was absorbed in another sentimental attachment. Moreover Mrs. Welsh, who snobbishly disliked Carlyle's simple origins, objected to a correspondence. Jane too continued to find his social awkwardness a drawback and taunted him humorously about it, which threw him into despair. A few months later, he prays her to "forget the roughness of my exterior if you think me sound within. . . . The Graces cannot live under a sky so gloomy and tempestuous as mine: I lament their absence since you lament it, but there is no remedy."

By the following spring, the prospective suitor Jane had been angling for had proved faithless and went abroad, and in spite of her mother's objections, she plunged into a course of reading under Carlyle's direction, though assuring him that her feelings could never be more than sisterly. He made no pretenses. He was now tutoring two boys in a wealthy family and still had no prospects, but she was the central fact in his life.

> The only thing I know is that you are the most delightful, enthusiastic, contemptuous, affectionate, sarcastic, capricious, warm-hearted, lofty-minded, half-angel, half-devil of a woman that ever ruled over the heart of man; that I will love you, must love you, whatever may betide, till the last moment of my existence.

It was five years after their first meeting before they married. A visit to London had convinced Carlyle that he could not work there, but he still had no steady employment in Scotland, though Jeffrey of the *Edinburgh Review* was interested in his work. Jane's letters can be shatteringly practical:

> Let me ask you, have you any *certain* livelihood to maintain me in the manner I have been used to live in? Any *fixed* place in the rank of society I have been born and bred in? No . . . as yet you have *not* attained them.

Nevertheless, he managed to kindle her faith in his future, and she soon conceded,

> According as my mind enlarges and my heart improves, I become more capable of comprehending the goodness and greatness which are in you, and my affection for you increases.

Indeed it was no mere flattery when she wrote this, and as she grew to love him, the more attractive she became. She had been a spoilt only child, and for all her charm and wit, had a hard streak of egotism. She was bright and acquisitive of ideas, but as intolerant as she was intelligent and had a great talent for mockery, which paralyzed her poor serious lover: "Do not laugh at me if you can help it; there is something in laughter that dries up all the channels of the heart." It was perhaps fortunate that Jane never did cease to make fun of Carlyle's "preaching vein," and his habit of becoming "sublime" in the style of a Minor Prophet; yet her belief in his genius was rooted solidly in her. As her love grew, she became humble: "You have loved me, not in blindness to my thousand faults, but in spite of them"; and when she describes her future husband to her aunt, she has no shadow of misgiving.

> He possesses all the qualities I deem essential . . . a warm true heart to love, a towering intellect to command me, and a spirit of fire to be the guiding star of my life.

Finally, practical matters were decided by Mrs. Welsh renting a small house for them in Edinburgh; a house with six rooms, Jane writes, "and more closets than I see the least occasion for unless you design to be another Bluebeard."

They settled most happily. But in spite of that, Edinburgh did not prove congenial to Carlyle's writing. The city atmosphere was too "cagelike" and after six months of it, they moved to Craigenputtock, a bleak farmhouse in Dumfries where they spent most of the next six years, and where Carlyle wrote *Sartor Resartus*. His brother looked after the farm, and Jane has a "perfect paragon" of a servant. Her early letters tell of her contentment in spite of their almost complete solitude: "My husband is as good company as reasonable mortal could desire." While he worked, she supervised the household, coped with the practical problems she always loved, and galloped over the moors on her pony.

But when Carlyle had finished *Sartor* he was restless to get out of "this almost ghastly solitude." He felt the book "will cause ears to tingle" if it could get a hearing, and to try and sell it, they decided to spend the winter of 1821–22 in London. Carlyle trudged around from publisher to publisher in vain, and tried to work on salable articles for magazines. They spent a few days with friends at Enfield and had a disastrous meeting with Charles Lamb. He was unfortunately quite tipsy, stammered out "a ghastly make-believe of wit," and was unforgivably rude. Highly amused at Jane's supper of porridge, he wanted to taste it and dipped his spoon in her bowl. Jane snapped out: "Your astonishment at my porridge cannot exceed my surprise at your manners." They were much more successful, however, in making friends with J. S. Mill, Leigh Hunt, and Crabb Robinson, and in seeing much of Jeffrey, who was doing his best to introduce Carlyle to editors.

They returned to Craigenputtock in the spring, but now its loneliness seemed unbearable. Carlyle longed for a library and for intellectual stimulus. Jane reported: "He is going mad for speech"; for her, the grim prospect of another winter there was frightful. Her own gaiety was quite eclipsed. She wrote to a cousin: "O Bess, for one good laugh with you for the sake of old times! I do not remember the time when I laughed." A short move to Edinburgh proved a failure and the following year they decided to go to London. Carlyle went ahead to find a house and settled on one at 5 Cheyne Row, Chelsea. He reported that it looked out on a row of old pollarded limes in front, and green hayfields at the back, and had a garden with a cherry and a walnut tree, where he could wander about in his dressing gown and smoke his pipe in peace. Fifty yards away was the busy water-front of the Thames, and finally, "Chelsea abounds more than any other place in omnibi."

In June 1834, with two hundred pounds as their entire capital, they settled in to what was to be their home for the rest of their lives. Jane flung herself into arrangements, and as she painted furniture, supped off porridge, saw the breadcrusts that her neighbors threw wastefully into the ashcans, and lent the feckless Mrs. Leigh Hunt, a few doors off, teacups, sugar, silver spoons and a brass fender, she congratulated herself on her Scottish "shiftiness" and thrift. Her dyed puce gown will do for the winter, with her "turned" pelisse, and she has smartened up the whole effect by a bonnet "with an air," having a little brown feather nodding over the front and a crown pointed like a sugar-loaf. The entertainment of friends at tea costs only a few pence, and if they go out themselves, clogs and the omnibi save the expense of a carriage.

Her economies were needful enough. Although *Sartor* had finally found a publisher, it found little favor with reviewers or readers, who criticized Carlyle's opinions as too mystical and his style as too turbulent. The market for his articles dried up, and he wrote in his journal in February 1835:

> It is now three and twenty months since I have earned one penny from the craft of literature. . . . To *ask* able editors to employ you will not improve, but worsen matters. You are like a spinster waiting to be married.

Their hopes were pinned to *The French Revolution,* the first volume of which was just completed after long labor. The two hundred pounds was very near its end, when that crushing catastrophe happened which appalls one afresh every time one thinks of it. Carlyle had lent the manuscript to J. S. Mill, and one evening, as Jane and Carlyle were sitting reading, Mill, "pale as Hector's ghost," burst in with the shattering news that the manuscript had been accidentally burnt. "It was like half-sentence of death to us both," said Carlyle, but "Oh, the burst of sympathy my poor darling then gave me!" More important than the burst of sympathy was the sustaining faith Jane gave him through the heartbreaking job of rewriting: "She burnt like a steady lamp beside me," he said. They borrowed a hundred pounds from Mill to keep going, but it was not until an evening in January 1837 that Carlyle put the completed manuscript of the three volumes into her hands and went out for a walk with that milestone behind him. After the publication, Carlyle's reputation was made; the early struggles were over. Not only were they out of what Carlyle called "the bewildering terror of coming to actual want of money," but he was a literary lion and Jane was a lion's wife. He was forty-one and she thirty-six.

There is a tenacious myth that the Carlyles were unhappily married: "this highly respectable, yet wofully mismated couple" as the *New York Herald* called them in a review of Mrs. Ireland's *Life of Jane Welsh Carlyle*, published in 1891. But that was before all the letters on both sides had been published, and now, with all the evidence in, it is impossible to agree with such a conclusion. We know Jane Carlyle better than any other English letter writer. We have an unbroken series of her letters from the age of eighteen to the very morning of her sudden death at sixty-five. The gaps are never for more than a few weeks, and the letters are a complete self-portrait and a continuing drama of married life. She was never one to be careful in the expression of her feelings; she was always spontaneous and impulsive. As she wrote to a young cousin, Jeanie Welsh: "I have got into the way of *splashing* off whatever is on my mind when I write to you, without forethought or backthought." She did the same with her husband, whether she was in good spirits or bad, full of affection or full of anger or full of self-pity. She was a volatile creature with extremes of all these; a complex personality of many moods: so loving and so cynical, so sympathetic and so harsh, so intolerant and so patient, so clear-sighted and so blind.

All these moods naturally affected her relations with her husband, but it is impossible to read her letters to him during their whole life together, even during the years of near estrangement, without recognizing the unbreakable bonds of deep understanding, trust and devotion between them. Take these passages from different decades. In 1837 she wrote to her mother-in-law:

> I have only him in the whole wide world to love me and take care of me, poor little wretch that I am. Not but what numbers of people love me after their fashion far better than I deserve; but then *his* fashion is so different from all these and seems alone to suit the sort of crotchetty creature that I am.

In 1844, she suspected that he is going to buy her a birthday present:

> Write me a longer letter than usual, and leave presents to those whose affection stands more in need of vulgar demonstration than yours does.

In 1863 she had a long and painful illness and had gone to the seaside to try and regain health:

> O my Dear! Shall I ever make fun for you again? . . . I want so much to *live*—and to be to you more than I have ever been. . . . I am terribly alone. But I don't want to interrupt your work.

Carlyle wrote to her continually in the same loving terms. But this is not to say that superficial storms were not frequent. Carlyle's life was centered in his writing, Jane's life was centered in him, and this in itself caused inevitable stresses and strains. She put her husband's work before any other consideration in her life, but that could not prevent her frequent bitter resentment of its claims. She once wrote grimly: "Harriet Martineau used to talk of writing being such a *pleasure* to her. In this house we should as soon dream of calling the bearing of children such a pleasure." Getting his books written meant to Carlyle untold—or rather very loudly told—struggle and travail. It threw him into "bewildered wrestlings"; a book, he said, was like a load of fire burning his heart, it roasted his life out until it was thrown out of him; his imagination was a black smithy of the Cyclops where his mind must work in continual darkness, broken only by lightnings. As Jane says on her side, the home atmosphere was full of sulphur and brimstone all the time. And these spells of creative activity would be interspersed with periods of the blackest depression, of what he himself called "sulky despair," full of egotistical lamentations and irritability, in whch he had no room to consider the needs of others. In one of these Jane writes that she is coming home from a visit in low spirits, and hopes to be cheered up. He replies:

> My poor Goody, depending on cheerful looks of *mine* for thy cheerfulness. How I love thee, it is not probable that thou or any mortal will know. But cheerful looks, when the heart feels slowly dying in floods of confusion and obstruction, are not the things I have to give.

When Jane is cheerful herself, she can make excellent comedy out of her trials as "a human partition" standing between a temperamental genius and an unsympathetic external world. She can work up brilliant extravaganzas of how she copes with landlords, tax assessors, demands for jury service, and more particularly with the eternal problem of distracting noises—girls playing the piano, howling dogs, crowing roosters and screaming parrots. Carlyle's personal nervous restlessness is vividly presented: moving around the house "like a sort of domestic Wandering Jew . . . lounging about from the mantelpiece to the table—from the table to the chairbacks—touching everything and contradicting everything"; or being so wild to get away and so incapable of making up his mind where he wants to go, "that living beside him has been like living the life of a weathercock in a high wind, blowing from all points at once." Or he returns home after she has had a tremendous housecleaning and rearranged everything for his comfort, only to be told after three days "he can neither think nor live with the rooms as they are" and so she finds herself "in the thick of a new mess":

> The carpets, which I had nailed down so well with my own hands, tumbled up again . . . and the prospects of new cleanings, new sewings, new arrangements, stretching away into eternity for anything I see.

No wonder that after this she declares defiantly: "I will lie on the sofa by heaven for two weeks and read French novels!"

For Jane could be as tempestuous as her husband, and if he was difficult to live with, so was she. She confesses herself "a brimstone of a creature," and one suspects that an entry in Carlyle's journal in 1840 tells of a common occurrence: "Work ruined for the day. Imprudently expressed complaints in the morning filled all the sky with clouds." Jane is excellent at giving good advice: "When one can only ray out darkness, best clap an extinguisher on yourself," but often she cannot follow it. Sometimes she is unforgivable in her own egotisms, and one wants to shake her! She will write a furiously angry letter one evening, "shrewing" her husband for changing plans and upsetting her own arrangements, find two letters from him next morning with full explanations and apologies, but conclude: "I must let the long letter I wrote yesterday go. . . . It is too much writing to throw away, after having given myself a headache over it." She can't resist wounding little jabs. When he writes a long letter about his doings and opinions, but not enough about *her,* she dismisses it: "It will read charmingly in your biography"; or she will describe a bad night: "Not what *you* call awake, that is, dozing, but broad wide awake." Moreover, not only did she write such jibes *to* him, she wrote them *of* him to others, a disloyalty of which he was never guilty. She will say she has a faceache, as the result of his insisting on her sitting in a draught on a train journey; or that no attention need be paid to any report he makes about her health, because as long as she can stand on her legs he never notices if anything is wrong with her. She jeers at his vanity: "With all his hatred of being made a lion of, he seems to tolerate those that make him so marvellously well"; and she suggests that it is for the same reason that he loves the attentions of their little dog:

> The infatuated little beast dances round him on its hind legs as I ought to do and can't; and he feels flattered and surprised by such unwonted capers to his honour and glory.

Much of this can no doubt be put down to ill-health. She wrote in 1846:

> Carlyle should have had a "strong-minded woman" for wife, with a perfectly sound liver, plenty of *solid fat,* and mirth and good humour without end.

They are too much alike, she thinks, especially as to their digestions and nervous systems, and so "we aggravate one another's tendency to despair." That many of Jane's physical symptoms were emotional in origin we cannot doubt, but they were none the less torturing for that. Even before her marriage we hear of her agonizing migraine headaches, which would last from twenty-four to sixty hours and leave her "all beaten into impalpable pulp." Her chronic digestive troubles, her sleeplessness and her depressions all sound as if they were the result of nervous stress, and the fact that they so often disappeared when she was happy and busy perhaps proves it. In spite of all her humorous or blistering accounts of the horrors of her household "earthquakes" during Carlyle's absences, she is never better than when she is having a "sack of Troy" in the home. She owns she finds it "rather inspiriting," and when the house is full of plasterers, plumbers, bricklayers, carpenters, painters, and paperhangers, she rigs up a gypsy tent in the garden with the "crumb-cloth" and the clothes props and sits there happily writing letters and making chair and sofa covers. The workmen arrive at six in the morning, but Jane, usually so full of complaints at being disturbed, comments only: "It makes a prodigious long day; but I do not weary, having so many mechanical things to do." Or again, she describes how one afternoon she is lying, a physical wreck, on the sofa, when an old beau of hers from Haddington days, walks in on her. They embrace and she is transformed:

> My bright, whole-hearted, impulsive youth seemed conjured back. . . . For certain my late deadly weakness was conjured away . . . dissolved in the unwonted feeling of gladness. I am a different woman this evening. I am well! I am in an atmosphere of *home* and *long ago*.

But a change of atmosphere in the immediate present has the same effect. Another day, in the same condition of lonely depression, Mrs. Macready (wife of the actor) persuades her to come to a party. It proved a very merry and wild affair, with Dickens performing conjuring tricks for the children, and "the gigantic Thackeray" capering like a Maenad, and much of Bohemian London playing the fool whole-heartedly far into the night. Jane describes it all with great gusto:

> And the result? Why, the result, my dear, was that I went to bed on my return and slept like a top!!! Plainly proving that excitement is my rest.

Perhaps that wasn't quite the right diagnosis, but that Jane lacked any regular pleasurable activity to absorb her nervous energies and take her mind off her many frustrations undoubtedly added much to her unhappiness and ill-health. The conventions of the day prevented women from pursuing many of the outlets we enjoy nowadays, but even so, Carlyle himself saw very clearly to the heart of her need. As early as 1842 he writes:

> My prayer is always and always has been that you would rouse up the fine faculties that *are* yours into some course of real true work, which you felt to be worthy of them and you! . . . I know well, none better, how difficult it all is,—how peculiar and original your lot looks to you, and in many ways *is*. . . . But I will never give up hope to see you adequately *busy* with your whole mind.

Jane too came to recognize the folly of centering her life on a husband whose engrossing interest was in his work. She writes bitterly in 1850:

> It is sad and wrong to be so dependent for the life of my life on any human being as I am on you; but I cannot by any force of logic cure myself at this date, when it has become second nature. If I have to lead another life in any of the planets, I shall take precious good care not to hang myself round any man's neck, either as a locket or a millstone.

No one knew better than she did herself how her extreme nervous sensibility handicapped her from taking a stable view of her matrimonial problems. When she is away in the summer of 1846 and thinks Carlyle has not written to her for her birthday, at once she falls into a frenzy of despair. She had gone confidently to the village post-office to fetch the letter and has been told it is not there:

> I walked back again, without speaking a word, and with such a tumult of wretchedness in my heart as you, who know me, can conceive. And then I shut myself up in my room to fancy everything that was most tormenting. Were you finally so out of patience with me you had resolved to write to me no more at all? Had you gone to Addiscombe and found no leisure there to remember my existence? Were you taken ill, so ill you could not write?

Carlyle's letter arrived, of course, the following day, but it is easy to see from her outburst here what is at the heart of her immediate trouble: "Had you gone to Addiscombe and found no leisure there to remember my existence?" For there was one long period in their married life when Jane, in addition to her usual despondencies, had progressively good reason for jealous misery.

It was in 1839 that Carlyle reported a dinner with "a certain Baring" and that he talked "a long long while" with the lady of the house, Lady Harriet Baring. He describes her as a "belle laide," but full of mirth and spirits, and one of the cleverest creatures he had ever met. The acquaintance, however, did not ripen until three years later, when Jane comments, in a letter to her cousin, Babbie Walsh, that her friend Geraldine Jewsbury is *scandalized* at the talk about it:

> For my part I am singularly inaccessible to jealousy, and am pleased rather that he has found *one* agreable house to which he likes to go and goes regularly . . . and then he visits them at their "farm" on Sundays, and are flights of charming little notes coming to create a pleasing titillation of the philosophic spirit!

But in the "little notes" Carlyle was sending Lady Harriet, he addresses her as "the daughter of the Sun," she has "the soul of a princess," she is "good and wise, beautiful and brave." Not that there was anything to be concealed. All three characters in the drama were middle-aged; Carlyle forty-nine, Jane forty-four and Lady Harriet a matronly thirty-seven. Yet the interrelations of a man with two such strong feminine personalities could hardly fail to be uneasy, and Jane had the worst of it. She had to live with Carlyle day in, day out, at the mercy of his moods, whereas to Lady Harriet he was always the worshiping admirer of her charms and sympathy. She had only to entertain and soothe him as hostess to guest.

For the first few years all Jane's references to Lady Harriet are extremely friendly. She describes her as "a very lovable spoilt child of Fortune," but her aristocratic prejudices are all that she criticizes. Otherwise she is "unquestionably very clever —just the wittiest woman I have seen" and "almost beautiful —simply through the intelligence and cordiality of her expression." On her first visit alone to the Barings in the country in 1845 she writes to her husband that she believes she will get along very well with her hostess, "altho' I can see that the Lady has a genius for ruling, whilst I have a genius for *not being ruled*."

The acquaintance soon ripened into affection on Jane's side.

She finds Lady Harriet "a grand woman every inch of her," sincere, graceful, amusing, and not in the least a coquette; "if all the men go out of their sober senses beside her, how can she help that?" Soon she is saying "I love her now as much as I *admired* her in the beginning." But the following summer she wrote the letter already quoted, though Carlyle's reply must have pleased her:

> By God's blessing, what of integrity and propriety there was in all this will one day become clear to all parties! Oh! to think that my affection for thee! . . . Adieu, my own Jane, whom nothing can divide from *me*.

Yet no doubt it did not please her that Carlyle went out of his way to see the Barings when he was in Scotland later in the summer, and it would have pleased her still less that he wrote to Lady Harriet that he would go twice as far "for one blink of your bonny face."

When November came, Lady Harriet's magic worked again. The Carlyles went to stay at Addiscombe, and Lady Harriet, obviously aware of Jane's jealousy, was evidently determined to show her how unnecessary it was. "I cannot make out what Lady Harriet is after," Jane writes. "To look at her one would say that she was systematically *playing my cards for me*." No doubt her hostess, with what Carlyle called her "divine benevolence," was doing exactly that. She let the parrot interrupt Carlyle's monologues and allowed him to meet "other little contradictions," while she does her best to flatter Jane into amiability. Jane almost ruefully admits her success, adding that she does not think a human being exists whom Lady Harriet could not charm if she wanted to. Other visits, however, were not so agreeable. On one Jane declares that her hostess evidently thinks her guest's ill-health is imaginary, and has tried to toughen her by not giving her a fire in her bedroom and offering no wine but hock which always upsets her. On another occasion Jane comes home after six weeks complaining that she is "so worn out with strenuous idleness as I do not remember ever to have been before." Carlyle, indeed, never did succeed in converting his "sovereign Lady," his "Daughter of the Harmonies" to any serious interests. He tried sending her Goethe and Sophocles and Seneca, but in 1849 (when Lady Harriet had become Lady Ashburton), Jane comments on his lack of progress:

> Mr. C. will never succeed in making her "more earnest," dear gay-hearted high-spirited woman that she is.

But this is the last agreeable reference Jane ever makes to her. Later in the same year she had an experience which, though she retails it with such spirit to her cousin, must have been most mortifying to her pride. The Carlyles were at a large party at Dickens' house:

> Before dinner old Rogers [Samuel Rogers, the poet] who ought to have been buried long ago . . . said to me: "I want to ask you; is your husband as infatuated as ever with Lady Ashburton? . . . Now tell me honestly is she kind to *you*—as kind as she is to your husband?"—"Why you know it is impossible for *me* to know *how* kind she is to my husband; but I can say that she is *extremely* kind to me" . . . "Well! it is very good of you to like her when she takes away all your husband's company from you. . . . Spends all his evenings with her, I'm told." "No, not all—you see he is here *this* evening." "Yes, I see he is here *this* evening—and *hear* him too—for he has done nothing but talk across the room since he came in." Very devilish old man! but he got no satisfaction to his devilishness out of *me*.

In private, though, Jane became more and more bitter. According to her letters she is made to suffer a series of insults. Carlyle is asked to join the Ashburtons for holidays and she is excluded; when Lady Ashburton comes to town for a few days, she has no time to visit the ailing Jane but asks Carlyle to dine at Bath House. Commenting on this to her cousin in 1851, she writes:

> I suppose I ought to feel by this time quite resigned . . . but I am angry and sorrowful. It is not of course any caprice *she* can show to me that annoys me. I have long given up the generous attempt at loving her. But it is to see *him* always starting up to defend everything she does or says, and no matter whether it be capricious behaviour towards his *wife*—so long as she flatters himself with delicate attentions.

In another letter in the same year, regretting that Babbie has decided to marry, she concludes: "But certainly I am not the best authorized person to tell people how they should manage their lives—having made such a mess of my own life—God help me!" Two years later it is Carlyle's turn to bewail *her* misunderstanding:

> Oh Jeannie, you know nothing of me just now. With all the clearness of vision you have, your lynx eyes don't reach into the inner region of me . . . what was always and will always be there. I wish you did. I wish you did.

As Jane's health and spirits became more miserable, Carlyle, now also sunk desperately in "The Valley of the Shadow of Frederick [the Great]," longs—very naturally, but not very tactfully—for escape to the stimulating and cheerful companionship of his Lady. Such times, he says, are "my little bit of earthly felicity . . . the brightest Star in all the week's firmament, perhaps the only star there." The climax of Jane's wretchedness came in 1855 when she kept the Journal which was to cause her husband such profound remorse when he found it after her death, and read of her agonies and repressions.

> Oct. 22. That eternal Bath House. I wonder how many thousand miles Mr. C. has walked between there and here . . . setting up always another milestone betwixt himself and me. Nov. 5. Alone this evening. Lady A. in town again; and Mr. C. of course at Bath House.

She is pathetic in her efforts to check her morbidity; trying to busy herself with practical things to give her mind no time to fester; mending Carlyle's dressing-gown to keep her heart from throbbing up into her head and maddening it; trying to tire herself with walking. When things seem more than she can bear, she tells herself to say over and over: "Look straight before you, Jane Carlyle. . . . Look above all at the duty nearest hand and what's more, do it."

A year later her emotional conflicts ended with the death of Lady Ashburton, and though some of her worst physical sufferings bedeviled her in the following years, and Carlyle's struggles with Frederick continued, the bitterness was gone, and her love and trust in her husband shines out in all her letters. When she died of a heart attack as she was driving alone in Hyde Park, Carlyle wrote the epitaph for her tombstone at Haddington.

> For forty years she was the true and ever-loving helpmate of her husband, and by act and word unweariedly forwarded him, as none else could, in all of worthy that he did or attempted. She died in London, 21st April 1866, suddenly snatched away from him, and the light of his life as if gone out.

Serving her husband's work, lovingly, humorously or grudgingly, certainly took first place in Jane's own existence, but it is time to see what made her "the light of his life" and gave her the reputation for the charm, warmth, vivacity, and wit described by so many of her circle, and which lives for us in the letters. Her correspondents were seldom people of any distinction—uncles, cousins, family friends, and in-laws form the bulk of them. To them all she recounts all the doings of her London life and the gossip about her London friends and acquaintances. She did the same to Carlyle at home in what she calls their Chelsean Nights Entertainments, when, after his working hours were over he would stretch himself on the hearthrug and smoke up the chimney ("if I were careful!" said Carlyle, describing such scenes), and she would lie on her sofa and give vivid accounts, grave or gay, of her own doings.

We come to know all her contradictory qualities. She had said when she was twenty-eight: "the only thing that makes one place more attractive to me than another is the quantity of *heart* I find in it," and that she had the warmest affections and most generous sympathies is clear enough. One friend called her "the most *concrete* woman" she knows, and her many practical kindnesses bear it out. In the early days in Edinburgh, when de Quincey fell ill—from a diet of seven wineglasses of laudanum a day, and all the game that went bad on the poulterer's hands, says Jane—she took him into their house and nursed him back to health. She declares that she has the same attraction for miserable people and mad people that amber has for straws. When a young German friend disappears, it is Jane who tracks him to the asylum where he has been taken, rescues him and cares for him until his friends can come from Germany. Again, when she finds a lost child in the street, she does not take her to the police station lest she should be frightened, but brings her home, leaving her address with the police, and keeps her fed and amused for five hours. If she catches some boys torturing "a little ugly brown bird," she immediately buys it from them for twopence and tries to save its life. She cannot understand how Lady Ashburton, who spends seven hundred pounds on a ball at Bath House, can be so stingy about her village children's party at The Grange. She spends only two pounds on forty-eight rubbishy presents: "I should have liked every child to have got at least a *frock* given it," Jane says indignantly.

She has indeed plenty of what she calls caustically "that damned thing, the milk of human kindness"; yet very close behind it is that disillusioned wry humor which causes her to comment on it in that way. She is often limited by her "concreteness." She is incapable of understanding any beliefs outside her own sturdy agnosticism, and like Carlyle himself, she has very little in the way of esthetic taste. She can appreciate George Eliot's deep humanity, and feels as a woman an affinity with Charlotte Brontë: "I perceive in her book so many things I have said myself." She can enjoy the social satire of *Vanity Fair,* but finds *David Copperfield* "arrant nonsense," Jane Austen "water-gruel for the mind," Browning "nothing but a fluff of feathers," and sees Taglione, the greatest ballet-dancer of the day, simply as "a woman, not even pretty, balancing herself on the extremity of one great toe, and stretching the other foot high into the air—much higher than decency ever dreamt of." But in spite of her rationalistic prejudices she has a refreshing intolerance of humbug. The barbarism of a fashionable wedding brings the comment: "All that senseless singing of *Te Deum* before the battle has begun!" and she disposes acidly of the cant that happiness is found in the happiness of others: "To eat a beefsteak when one is hungry yields a satisfaction of a much more positive character than seeing one's neighbour eat it."

She was by no means one of those who see only the best in others; but then those people are not often the best company, and Jane is very good company. She rings a bell in many memories when she describes a dinner with some very dull acquaintances:

> It's like seasickness: one thinks at the time one will never risk it again, and then the impression wears off and one thinks perhaps one's constitution has changed and that this time it will be more bearable.

Or the account of a visit to the country rectory where Regy Buller, the dullest of the two brothers whom Carlyle had tutored during their courtship, now holds the living. It is all so vividly deadly: the daily drive with old Mrs. Buller, the nightly game of chess with old Mr. Buller, the mouldering church—" anything so like the burial place of revealed religion you have never seen—nor a rector more fit to read the burial service." When Sunday comes, she has to listen to the "imbecilities" of Regy's sermon, which goes on "like the cawing of rooks," and to his giving out the psalm "in a loud, sonorous, perfectly

Church of England tone." And since it is a day of rest, the carriage horses are only *walked* "on principle."

Yet all this satirical exaggeration was part of the vivacity which was one of her great attractions. She never lost her zest for life in spite of all her miseries. When at the age of fifty-two she finds "Scotch-looking snow" in the street on coming home from the theatre, she reports that she was so "drunk" with the sensation that she ran along the street with her bonnet hanging down her back, one minute taking a slide and the next lifting a handful of snow to eat it! Or she is glad she was persuaded to get an evening dress," cut down to the due pitch of indecency" to go to a ball at Bath House, "not for any pleasure I had at the time, being past dancing and knowing but few people—but it is an additional idea for life to have seen such a party."

She never had conventional beauty, but was always "that very elegant creature" that Anne Thackeray found her in her sixties; always slim and alert, with a fragile body and colorless face, abundant black hair never touched with gray and expressive dark eyes which could be either tender or mischievous: "a face full of intellect and kindness blended gracefully and lovingly together" as one of her men friends described it. "Shall I ever make fun for you again" she said pathetically to her husband in a letter already quoted, and jokes flew about at Cheyne Row. Indeed Tennyson made a very shrewd remark when he said that no couple who chaffed one another as heartily as the Carlyles could possibly be unhappily married. Jane is full of good-natured mischief. In a gay mood she fetches a supply of light French novels from the London Library, but "having still however some sense of decency remaining" she reports that she signed in the ledger for them "Erasmus Darwin"; or she creates a ridiculous picture of herself riding up the Malvern Hills with Old Sterling, leader writer to *The Times:* "each on a live donkey! Just figure it! With a Welsh lad whipping us from behind; for they were the slowest of donkeys, though named, in defiance of all probability, *Fly* and *Lively*." She confesses to nervousness lest Carlyle will address his lecture audience: "Fool creatures come here for diversion," instead of "Ladies and Gentlemen," and wonders if the best way to stop him at the end will be to have a lighted cigar laid on the desk as the clock strikes four. Carlyle of course is in the letters as vividly as herself—with pellets of cotton, with which he has hopefully plugged his ears, sticking at the end of some stray hairs; or in uncongenial company looking like a chained tiger; or setting out with three maps of Great Britain and two of the world in his pocket, to find a house within twenty miles of London; or with clumsy tenderness, presenting her with a cloak he has chosen himself: "not *very* ugly, only entirely unsuitable to the rest of my habiliments, being a brownish colour with orange spots."

We meet many of the great names of the age in what she describes as "our long, dimly-lighted, perfectly neat and quaint room." Tennyson, embarrassed to find Carlyle is out, but wooed out of his shyness by Jane getting out pipes and tobacco, brandy and water, with the triumphant result that he stayed "for three mortal hours—talking like an angel—only exactly as if he were talking with a clever *man*, which strained me to a terrible pitch of intellectuality"; Browning, asked to put the kettle back on the hob and depositing it on the hearth-rug while he went on with his conversation; George Eliot, "with her look of Propriety personified, and oh, so *slow!*" Harriet Martineau holding up her ear-trumpet to Carlyle "with a pretty, blushing air of coquetry"; Carlyle expounding the Schleswig-Holstein question "from a few hundred years before the beginning of it" to poor Mrs. Oliphant, who had to sit like a passive bucket being pumped into; or Macaulay, beating even Carlyle himself as a talker—"in quantity," adds Jane loyally.

Or we catch cosy intimate glimpses of Jane with her particular friends. She and Mazzini, their feet on the fender, regaling themselves with wine, figs, and gingerbread; or Erasmus Darwin (elder brother of Charles), having heard Mazzini say that Jane should wear a shawl, returning next day with "an immense gauze-looking shawl of white lambswool"; or gossiping with Mrs. Macready over Harriet Martineau's novel *Deerbrook:*

> She asked me how I liked Harriet's book. I answered "How do *you* like it?" She made wide eyes at me and drew her little mouth toegether into a button. We both burst out laughing and that is the way to get fast friends.

Some readers claim that the letters are too full of health, servants and domestic difficulties, that they are as a friend of Jane Austen said of *Emma,* "too natural to be interesting." But Jane's talent was, in its small way, like that of her greater namesake, to transform the commonplace. Even her complaining is vivid: lying sleepless in misery "pitted against chaos" and coming off second best; or listening to a barking dog until the universe seems one great dog-kennel; or, more cheerfully, on the way to convalescence, "not quite well yet—at least, I am still wearing signals of distress, a nightcap and shawl—partly, I confess, from a secret persuasion that these equipments render my appearance more interesting." Or who can find it dull to visualize a housecleaning with the tables and chairs "all with their legs in the air, as if in convulsions"; or to hear of the applicant for a job who recommended herself by declaring: "When people die, I can lay 'em out perfect."

When the first edition of the *Letters and Memorials* was published in 1883, Jane's unconventionality was deplored. Her jokes about blue pills and bedbugs upset the reviewers, and as one American critic remarked: "Whatever else she was, she was manifestly no lady." Not only did she make unseemly jokes, but her standards of ladylike refinement and language were low. She refused to wear a crinoline, she lunched alone in restaurants and rode on the top of omnibuses, and on being accosted in the street, merely said "Idiot," and passed on with no shrinking panic. She starts a letter to a neglectful friend: "Why the devil don't you write?" and on a dull visit to the country heads her letter, in place of address: "Hell." But it is all this which makes her the most unaffected of letter-writers; so gusty and vivid, "splashing off" whatever she has to say, with such natural vitality and phrasing—whether she is sending Carlyle a howl from the midst of a household "earthquake" to stop his brother from coming to stay: "For God's sake don't let John plump in upon me in my present puddlement," or describing one of her own moods of angry misery: "the mind of me all churned into froth," or picturing herself coming home from a few days at an Inn in the Isle of Wight: "I looked (and felt) as if just returned from the Thirty Years War. Sleepless, bug-bitten, bedusted and bedevilled." Letters, she said, were a poor substitute for a warm, breathing personality: "One cannot, in writing, eke out one's words with tones of the voice—looks, gestures, an occasional *groan,* an occasional kiss!" Yet she can make her charm glow through her words; in a greeting: "I kiss you from ear to ear"; in a bantering signature: "Your adorable wife"; in an opening reminder: "Now stop! Have you eaten your breakfast? If not, eat it: the letter will not cool by keeping—the tea and toast will!"

Jane Carlyle's letters are so spontaneous and uninhibited that inevitably we know the worst as well as the best of her. But there is no doubt which tips the balance. She can be jealous, neurotic, self-complacent and malicious. At times we can think of her in the words of Charlotte Cushman, the American actress, who found her "that plain, keen, unattractive and yet inescapable woman." But how much more often she is generous, witty, entertaining and lovable. To Carlyle she may have been all that her epitaph said, as wife and helpmate to a man of genius; to her friends, and to her sympathetic readers, more of her essential impulsive warmth was caught by Leigh Hunt in his well-known little poem. He had been sick for some time and came to call on his recovery. Jane welcomed him with a heartfelt embrace.

> Jenny kissed me when we met,
>     Jumping from the chair she sat in;
> Time, you thief, who love to get
>     Sweets into your list, put that in!
> Say I'm weary, say I'm sad,
>     Say that health and wealth have missed me,
> Say I'm growing old, but add
>     Jenny kissed me.

# Edward FitzGerald

1809-1883

THE RELATIONSHIP between Edward FitzGerald and Thomas Carlyle epitomizes so much of FitzGerald's characteristic qualities that it is perhaps as good an introduction as any to the letters of that shy, eccentric, yet highly individual personality. He and Carlyle met in 1842 when Carlyle was forty-seven and FitzGerald thirty-three, and their friendship lasted until Carlyle's death thirty-nine years later. Thackeray took FitzGerald to Chelsea on his first visit and his guest was not prepared to find his host very congenial. He did not admire *The French Revolution*, and had found *Heroes and Hero-worship* "perfectly insane." Carlyle was at work on his *Cromwell* and had recently visited the battlefield of Naseby. In the course of the conversation FitzGerald happened to mention that Naseby was one of his family's estates, and that he thought Carlyle had been misled as to the exact site of the battle by an obelisk put up in the wrong place by FitzGerald's father. He had himself done some investigation of the history and local traditions, and was pretty sure he had proof for his own findings. This was the start of a long correspondence and FitzGerald was very active in supervising excavations and reconstructing the facts. However, on the publication of Carlyle's book in 1845, FitzGerald wrote to another friend, with rather natural irritation: "Carlyle has entirely mis-stated all about Naseby, after all my trouble."

FitzGerald continued to visit Cheyne Row when he was in

London, though his youthful gaiety pained his host. After an evening there, FitzGerald reports:

> An organ was playing a polka even so late in the street: and Carlyle was rather amazed to see me polka down the street. He shut the door with a kind of groan . . .

Five years later FitzGerald reports of another visit: "He lectured without intermission for three hours . . . and I was very glad to get away." In 1855 Carlyle paid a short visit to the Suffolk farmhouse where FitzGerald was then living, but it was not repeated, and as FitzGerald had then given up visits to London, they did not meet again during the remaining twenty-three years of Carlyle's life. FitzGerald was embarrassed after writing a yearly letter to his old friend at the end of 1865, with greetings to his wife, to hear that she had died "in a very tragical way" in April, and that he had heard nothing of it, since he did not read the London newspapers. Five years later he writes nostalgically of the past:

> Many pleasant evenings do I remember . . . cups of tea made by her that is gone; and many a pipe smoked with you in your little garden.

In 1873, Charles Eliot Norton gave a copy of the Rubáiyát of Omar Khayyám to Carlyle and asked him if he could by any chance verify that the anonymous translation (published originally in 1859) was by a Reverend Edward FitzGerald, "who lived somewhere in Norfolk and was fond of boating." Carlyle wrote to FitzGerald, calling the book "a kind of jewel in its way," and expressing his amazement at discovering that "the complete silence and unique modesty in regard to said meritorious and successful performance, was simply a feature of *my own Edward FitzGerald.*"

In 1876, FitzGerald was glad to subscribe to a medallion for Carlyle's eightieth birthday, but criticized the Address that went with it and thought Carlyle might have declined the reference it contained to his "life of Heroism":

> I have no doubt he would have played a brave man's part if called on, but meanwhile he has only sat pretty comfortably at Chelsea, scolding all the world for not being heroic, and not always very precise in telling them how . . .

But on the publication by Froude of Carlyle's *Reminiscences* after his death two years later, he exclaims:

> How is it I did not know that Carlyle was so good, grand and even lovable . . . he never spoke of himself in that way . . . I regret that I did not know what the book tells us (about his early life), that I might have loved him as well as admired him.

The following year he was much shocked at *The Letters and Memorials of Jane Welsh Carlyle.* He passes no judgment on the quality of the letters, but only on their publication:

> I am reading *Jane Carlyle* with *his* 'Elucidations'—deeply interesting both in their several ways, but whether such life-long suffering on one side, and repentance at having overlooked it on the other, be quite proper for the public eye, is another question—But—brave old Carlyle!

A few months later he had to go to London on business and went to see the Carlyle statue on the Chelsea Embankment, and the old house in Cheyne Row, which he had not visited for twenty-five years:

> No. 5 . . . which had cost her so much, her life, one may say, to make habitable for him, now all neglected, unswept, ungarnished, uninhabited, "TO LET." I cannot get it out of my head, the tarnished scene of tragedy (one must call it) there enacted.

This little sketch omits two most important aspects of FitzGerald's personality: his capacity for strong affection, and his love of the Suffolk countryside and seacoast. But it illustrates very well his mixture of sustained loyalty to his friends with outspoken criticism of them; his early withdrawal from direct personal contacts and from any social or literary relationships in London and his almost pathological refusal to tell any but a very few intimates of his own literary work. He was indeed, as Fanny Kemble said of him, a man "who took more pains to avoid fame than others do to seek it." He destroyed almost all his letters from Carlyle, Tennyson and Thackeray, because "I would not leave anything of private, personal history behind me, lest it should fall into some unscrupulous hand." The idea that others kept *his* letters and that he would be remembered not only as the translator of Omar Khayyám but as one of the best of letter-writers would probably have given him more pain than pleasure. His early editors, however, in their anxiety to be discreet, suppressed a great deal in them. Much unpublished material still remains in the library of Trinity College, Cambridge and elsewhere, and no complete edition has yet been published.*

None of FitzGerald's oddities, however, appeared in his early days. His parents both came from old aristocratic and wealthy Irish families. His father's name was Purcell, but when his mother inherited a very large estate in Ireland the family took her name. His mother seems to have been a very handsome and a very dominating woman, who liked to live ostentatiously, dining off gold plate and driving about behind four black horses. Her eight children, three sons and five daughters, stood in awe of her. Edward was the third son and seventh child. Why the FitzGeralds chose to settle in Suffolk is not known; they had already a house in London, a large Irish estate and three other English ones. No doubt all those properties and possessions had much to do with FitzGerald's dislike of the moneyed classes and his determination to ignore and repudiate them—though not to the extent of ever earning his own living!

His childhood seems to have been very happy. The children were evidently left very much to themselves. Reminiscing to

* Professor Alfred McK. Terhune prints a good number of unpublished letters in his biography. I have quoted from some of them with his permission.

Fanny Kemble in 1872, FitzGerald says he remembered watching his father going hunting, from the nursery windows, and adds: "My mother used to come up sometimes and we children were not much comforted." The family moved to Paris for five years when Edward was nine years old, and returned to put the boys in school at Bury St. Edmunds. The headmaster instilled a love of the classics and of English literature in his pupils, which Edward never lost. He also made lifelong friends there: W. B. Donne, a descendant of the poet and relative of Cowper, later librarian of the London Library and Licenser of Plays; James Spedding, from a wealthy Cumberland family, who held some minor Government offices, but spent most of his life on a biography of Bacon; John Kemble, son of the actor Charles Kemble, and brother of Fanny, with whom FitzGerald corresponded regularly in later life. From school he went to Trinity College, Cambridge, where again he made some lifelong friends: John Allen, later an Archdeacon; W. H. Thompson, afterwards Master of Trinity; and dearest of all to him at that time, Thackeray. Tennyson he knew only by sight, "a sort of Hyperion," but he did not meet him till some years later.

On leaving Cambridge, he and Thackeray spent some months together in Paris, but he was already, at the age of twenty-one, planning his withdrawal from social contacts. He wrote to Allen:

> I cannot stand seeing new faces in polite circles. You must know I am going to become a great bear: and have got all sorts of Utopian ideas into my head about society: these may all be very absurd, but I try the experiment on myself, so I can do no great hurt.

He combined these asocial ideas, however, with a deep emotional involvement with his friends. So far as we know FitzGerald lived a completely sexless life, but as he said himself, some of his friendships "were more like loves," and all his special friends were men. To Allen he wrote in 1832:

> I have such a love of you, and of myself, that once every week, at least, I feel spurred on by a sort of gathering up of feelings to vent myself in a letter upon you.

He insists that Allen need not answer: "You, who do not love writing, cannot think that anyone else does—but I am sorry to say that I have a very young-lady-like partiality to writing to those I love."

At the same time he is pleading with Thackeray: "I see so few people I care about, and so, Oh Willy, be constant to me." But already he feels that perhaps writing is safer than meeting: in letters "there are no blue-devilish moments: one of us isn't kept waiting for the other, there are no disappointments with one another causing flatness and disgust." He concludes in good spirits, though, enclosing a set of bad, but obviously heartfelt verses on their perfect friendship. Thackeray responded to his "Teddibus" with equal warmth. Thackeray went to Paris to study art in 1832, and for a while there was a dream that they should share a decayed château in Normandy and live "after the manner of Pylades and Orestes." But by 1835 Thackeray was deep in his courtship of Isabella Shawe and the following year he had married. He then urges FitzGerald to come to Paris, exclaiming a little insensitively: "It would do your heart good to see how happy I am."

It was in the nature of things that all FitzGerald's friends married and set out on careers of their own, which inevitably weakened early intimacies. A few years later, however, he proved his staunch loyalty to Thackeray through all the strain of his wife's mental illness, helping him with money and encouragement. But then Thackeray's fame divided them again. FitzGerald rated most of Thackeray's work very highly, but he felt he had become a social climber and dependent on flattery: "He must have got surrounded with a set of praise-plasterers, so as scarce to be able to breathe without it." In 1852, however, Thackeray wrote to FitzGerald before sailing for a lecture tour in America, addressing him as "My dearest old friend," asking him to be his literary executor if anything happened to him, and saying, "I should like my daughters to know that you are the best and oldest friend their father ever had." FitzGerald responded with all his old affection:

> I truly believe there is no man alive loves you (in his own way of love) more than I do . . . [but] we live in such different worlds: and it is almost painful to me to tease anybody with my seedy dullness, which is just bearable by myself. Life every day seems a more total failure and mess to me: . . . I am become a sad Epicurean—just desirous to keep on the windy side of bother and pain.

But this rebirth of affection was left at that exchange of letters. They never met again, though FitzGerald wrote to Donne on the news of Thackeray's sudden death in 1864:

> I wish he were alive that I might write and tell him how the Newcomes were illuminating my long evenings. But if he were alive, I don't think he would care to be told so by me now; I think he had ceased to remember me; and I'm sure I can't wonder.

It is sad that he did not know that, as reported later by Anne Thackeray, when she asked her sick father which of his friends he cared for most, he replied: "Why, dear old Fitz to be sure."

Much the same pattern repeated itself with Tennyson. FitzGerald greatly admired the poems of 1832, but did not meet the poet until 1835, at Spedding's home in Cumberland. Then he was enthusiastic: "The more I have seen of him, the more cause I have to think him great." He felt "the universality of his mind," and there was "much sitting up till two or three in the morning with pipes in our mouths." Spedding and FitzGerald were both sons of wealthy parents, but Tennyson was not and was nevertheless determined to devote himself to poetry. FitzGerald offered financial help at any time and it may have been taken in the following lean years as help towards the publication of the 1842 volume. But again success and marriage changed the picture and as usual FitzGerald refused to subordinate his critical sense to friendship. As Tennyson's successive volumes appeared, he became increasingly disappointed: "none of the old champagne flavour." *The Princess* seemed to him "a wretched waste of power at a time of life when a man ought to be doing his best": "I almost feel hopeless about Alfred now." *In Memoriam* "is full of the finest things, but it is monotonous and has that air of being evolved by a Poetical Machine of the highest order." FitzGerald visited the Tennysons two or three times but, as with Thackeray, he flinched from their living "on a somewhat large scale, with perpetual visitors," and gave it up when he was forty-five, though he continued to correspond warmly. Over twenty years later, Mrs. Tennyson reported to him that her husband had read and much admired the Rubaíyát. FitzGerald was amazed and delighted: "To think of Alfred approving my old Omar! I never should have thought he even knew of it. Certainly I should never have sent it to him." In September 1876, FitzGerald's housekeeper at Woodbridge, brought him a calling card on which was written: "Dear old Fitz—I am passing thro' and am here." It was Tennyson with his son Hallam. "We fell at once into the old humour," FitzGerald wrote to Fanny Kemble, "as if we had only been parted twenty days instead of so many years." FitzGerald was still ungracious about the later poems: "I did not ask to hear anything of them—for indeed I think he might as well ship his oars now—I was even impious enough to tell him so." However, Hallam left a charming picture of them talking together under a tree in the garden, FitzGerald "affectionate, genial and humorous, with his gray, floating locks, sitting among his doves, which perched about him on head and shoulder and knee, and cooed to him as he sat in the sunshine, beneath the roses." Tennyson embodied the scene in some verses "To E. FitzGerald" in his volume *Tiresias,* but they appeared after Fitz's death. When Tennyson had news of that, he wrote: "I had no truer friend: he was one of the kindest of men, and I have never known one of so fine and delicate a wit."

In 1835, when FitzGerald was twenty-six, there was a period when it looked as if he, like all his friends, would fall in love and abjure his bachelor freedom. He wrote to Thackeray:

> . . . and now, my Dear Boy, do you be very sensible, and tell me one thing—think of it in your bed, and over your cigar . . . shall I marry? I vow to the Lord that I am upon the brink of saying 'Miss—do you think you could marry me?' to a plain, sensible girl without a farthing.

He owns that she may refuse him, since she is very pious and her father regards him as a pagan. To Allen a few months later he writes in high spirits—feels inclined to dance around his room, in fact, because his lady is again staying at his parents' house and "I like her more than ever." She has humour and sense, is healthy and a good walker and gardener, is fond of the country and understands housekeeping and children. But then he concludes:

> Ay, there's the rub. Should I dance round my room . . . if I were married and had seven children? Answer me that.

The young lady was Elizabeth Charlesworth, daughter of the rector of a village outside Ipswich, and ten years later she was to marry Edward Cowell, the young man fourteen years her junior who introduced FitzGerald to Persian poetry. Though apparently FitzGerald never did bring himself to a proposal, he remained devoted to her, and both she and her husband were among his closest friends. He sent some of her verses to Thackeray in 1852: "made years ago by the little Suffolk woman . . . who would have been my Poetry if I had had wit enough."

What was the life he chose instead, which involved giving up sociable contacts with his friends and the common pleasures and pains of family life? For some years after leaving Cambridge he continued to live with his family, but made frequent visits to London. There he took rooms near the British Museum and spent happy days seeing his friends, buying books and pictures and going to galleries, theaters, and concerts. In the summer he paid long visits to Gelderstone Hall, near Beccles, the home of a married sister. He describes himself there, to Allen, in 1839, spending the morning reading Tacitus; lunching on cream cheese and fruit; then going for a ride; then weeding the lawn:

> And then, coming in, I sit down to write to you, my sister winding red worsted from the back of a chair, and the most delightful little girl in the world chattering incessantly. . . . Such as life is, I believe I have got hold of a good end of it.

Another friend with whom he spent happy times was William Browne, whom he had met on a visit to Allen in Wales, and who lived near Bedford. Browne was eight years younger than himself, "full of confidence, generosity and the glorious spirit of youth." He had no intellectual tastes, which sometimes irritated FitzGerald, but loved outdoor sports and returned FitzGerald's affection warmly. He stayed often at Browne's country house: they would ride, or fish "and have tea in a pothouse and so walk home . . . it's all deuced pleasant." But marriage again intervened, though FitzGerald made great friends with Mrs. Browne and continued to visit the family until Browne was fatally injured in a fall from his horse in 1860.

In his late twenties FitzGerald moved from the family home at Boulge Hall to a dilapidated cottage at the gates of the estate, and before he was thirty he had settled into the self-centered, sedentary existence which was to last for the rest of his life. He does not approve of himself: "I scorn my nerveless carcass more and more every day—but there's no good in talking." He knows that "men ought to have an ambition to stir and travel and fill their heads and senses," but his "besetting indolence" prevents it. He continues to describe himself as "leading a life of my usual vacuity," or "given over to turnips and inanity."

> A little more folding of the hands—the same faces—the same fields—the same thoughts occurring at the same turns of the road—this is all I have to tell of . . . but the summer gone.

But he declares he has "a talent for dullness," or again: "Travelling, you know, is vanity. The soul remains the same." London, he comes to feel "melts away all individuality into a common lump of cleverness . . . I can still find the heart of England beating healthily down here." He prefers the Suffolk countryside to the beauties of Italy:

> Boulge is one of the ugliest places in England—one of the dullest—it has not the merit of being bleak on a grand scale—it has the compensation of rich meadow lands full of flowers and the slow stream of the river Deben winding to its estuary.

Its very monotony is one of its charms to him, where "every winding of the river, every church spire, every country pot-house and the quality of its beer," is already well-known. His own existence repeats itself daily:

> I read of mornings; the same old books over and over again, having no command of new ones; walk with my great black dog of an afternoon, and at evening sit with open windows up which China roses climb, with my pipe, while the black-birds and thrushes begin to rustle bedwards in the garden, and the nightingale to have the neighbourhood to herself.

"How old to tell of, how new to see!" he exclaims of the clouds, the flowers, the trees, the grass "striving with the buttercups." Or he will go out in the garden before going to bed and listen to the continuous moaning sound, "which I know to be, not an infant exposed, or a female ravished, but the sea more than ten miles off."

But the winter does not sound so pleasant. In February 1844 he reports that he has had three influenzas:

> But this is no wonder: for I live in a hut with walls as thin as a sixpence: windows that don't shut: a clay soil safe beneath my feet: a thatch perforated by lascivious sparrows over my head. Here I sit, read, smoke, and become very wise . . .

The influenzas cannot have been very serious, as he wrote to Fanny Kemble when he was sixty-five that bronchitis had kept him in for a week and "I have not been shut up indoors for some fifty-five years—since measles at school."

George Crabbe, grandson of the poet, whose father was rector of a neighboring parish said that at thirty-six FitzGerald looked "a grave middle-aged man: never seemed very happy or lighthearted, though his conversation was most amusing sometimes. He did not visit with the neighbouring gentlefolks, as he hated a set dinner party." He cared nothing for appearances. A visitor to the cottage describes being met by his host in dressing gown and slippers,

> pictures standing against the walls—books, sticks, music, scattered about on the tables, chairs and floor. An open piano . . . lumber everywhere . . .

Meanwhile, two other friends he made near his Suffolk home were to bring unexpected results into his life. Bernard Barton, the Quaker poet and friend of Charles Lamb, lived, with his daughter Lucy, at Woodbridge, the small country town near Boulge. Since Barton was one of the few men in the neighborhood who shared FitzGerald's bookish and artistic interests, it was natural that they should meet frequently. Barton's position as clerk in a bank brought in very little money and FitzGerald supplemented it with an income of £300 a year. Some of Fitz's most charming letters were written to Barton, and he enjoyed the suppers of toasted cheese and tea or beer which Lucy provided for their evening entertainment. A much greater intellectual stimulus, however, came from a meeting, probably in 1845, with Edward Cowell, of Ipswich. Cowell was then a young man of twenty, a brilliant linguist, whose father's death had forced him to leave school at sixteen and go into the family business. But he had continued to study languages, and with the help of a retired Indian army officer, had added Persian and Sanskrit to the classical and European languages he had already mastered. He and FitzGerald probably met at the home of Elizabeth Charlesworth, whose father was vicar of a village outside Ipswich. The following year, Cowell married Elizabeth and settled in the neighboring village of Branford, where FitzGerald was a frequent visitor. In later years he refers constantly to those happy years, to the creeper-covered cottage, the old-fashioned garden, and above all to the companionship in sociability and scholarship. For Cowell fired FitzGerald first to study Spanish, so that later he translated and published six of the plays of Calderón, and then Persian. The happy years, probably the happiest of FitzGerald's life, ended in 1851, when Elizabeth was determined that any future for her husband in scholarship depended on his getting a degree at Oxford. FitzGerald fought against the idea with a force he never showed about anything else. Elizabeth wrote to a sympathetic friend that "in the dreadfully long letters E.F.G. is rousing up his languid energies to send us," he was distorting the picture of university life, so that her husband, who was just beginning "to my heartfelt thankfulness to *rise* to the occasion . . . is now almost wholly turned back again." Elizabeth won, however, and it was while he was at Oxford that Cowell discovered in the Bodleian Library "some curious infidel and Epicurean tetrastichs by a Persian of the eleventh century." These were the Rubáiyát or quatrains of Omar Khayyám. Cowell copied the verses and sent them to FitzGerald.

In 1849 Bernard Barton died. FitzGerald wrote to Donne: "We do not yet know what Miss Barton will have or what else she is to do with herself." He calls her "poor thing," and soon tells of the plan to publish by subscription *Selections from the Poems and Letters of Bernard Barton,* edited by his Daughter, to which he was to contribute a preface. As usual with his friends, FitzGerald was loyal and admiring of the man, but quite uncompromising about Barton as a poet: "he was not fastidious about exactness of thought or of harmony of numbers." No doubt FitzGerald footed the bill for the volume and no doubt also he had promised Barton that he would provide for Lucy, and proposed continuing the same income he had given her father. No direct evidence exists as to what happened. The general opinion is that Lucy declared it would be improper for her to take money from anyone not her husband, and that she so worked on FitzGerald's chivalry that he felt he must offer her marriage.

No one could suppose that FitzGerald, who could not bring himself to propose to Elizabeth Charlesworth, who attracted him so strongly, would take the initiative with Lucy Barton. She was unattractive physically: others describe her as tall and masculine-looking, with heavy features and a loud voice. FitzGerald hardly mentions her in his letters to her father, and never to anyone else. But nevertheless there seems to have been some sort of engagement dating from soon after Barton's death. Probably FitzGerald felt more or less safe in the fact that certainly his mother would not approve the match and that he was entirely dependent on her for his income. Lucy took a position as companion to the daughters of some wealthy Quakers in Norfolk. But in 1855 Mrs. FitzGerald died suddenly, and the following year FitzGerald was breaking the news of his approaching marriage to his friends. "A very doubtful experiment," he writes to one, "I shut my eyes to the consequences." To another: "I am going to be married—don't congratulate me!" To Allen: "Thank Mrs. Allen for her sanguine wishes—sanguiner than my expectations." To his misery was added the further unhappiness that Cowell had accepted a position at the University of Calcutta. He and his wife sailed for India in August, and FitzGerald could not face seeing them "to say a Goodbye that costs me so much." He was married in November at Weymouth, the home of some Barton relatives. No member of the FitzGerald family was present. Someone wrote later: "On the fateful day he looked like a victim being led to his doom. He walked as one walking in his sleep, mute and with head bowed." In fact the only remark noted is that at the wedding breakfast, on being offered some blancmange, he shuddered and said: "Ugh! congealed bridesmaid!"

The outcome was what might be expected. They were both forty-eight years old to start with. Then Lucy had a dominating nature, and her tastes had changed during her years in the society of wealthy people. She was quite sure she could bully FitzGerald into taking the social position she wished for herself. They took rooms in London. Sir Frederick Pollock, a noted lawyer, afterwards described an evening visit to them with his wife:

> The wretchedness of the terrible mistake he had made was apparent all the time, and on leaving his own place he came away with us very much the worse for some wine he had been taking, a condition in which I never saw him at any other time.

In a letter to Donne, he describes their gloomy sitting-room, and says brutally of his wife: "My Contemporary looks in this Chamber of Horrors like Lucrezia Borgia." In the summer they went to Yarmouth and from there FitzGerald wrote to Cowell that he longed to get on a ship and "never see land again till I saw the mouth of the Ganges, and there live what remains of my shabby life." George Borrow, who lived near and visited them, reported also that his host got drunk and on the walk home with him lay down on the roadside and went to sleep there.

They separated in August, at FitzGerald's insistence no doubt, and he gave her a generous income. Writing to the Cowells, he calls the marriage "a rash act," which, "had good sense and experience prevailed . . . would never have been completed." But he owns: "I am very much to blame, both on the score of stupidity in taking such a step, and want of courageous principle in not making the best of it when taken." At the same time he knows that she is far better off without him, and is now free to live her own life, "while I am creeping out of the world in my own way."

But the marriage had one very fortunate consequence. In the spring of 1857, in the midst of his emotional and nervous misery, FitzGerald turned to the Persian quatrains that Cowell had sent him the year before. "Omar" he writes to Cowell, "breathes a sort of consolation to me." When he left his wife for a visit to Browne in June, he "put away all books except Omar Khayyám, which I could not help looking over in a paddock covered with buttercups and brushed by a delicious breeze." In the same month he received a second and rather different transcript of the poem which Cowell had found in a library in Calcutta, which quickened his interest still further. The following month, in the garden of his sister's house, full of roses "blowing as in Persia," one of the quatrains formed itself into English in his mind.

FitzGerald flamed into creative activity; he became "Edward FitzOmar" and worked for six months on the translation. When the editor of *Fraser's Magazine* asked him for a contribution, he sent thirty-five of the "less wicked" quatrains for his approval, adding however that they might be "rather dangerous" for his clerical public. The editor evidently agreed, for he did not print them, and eighteen months later FitzGerald asked for them back. He then added forty more stanzas and decided to publish the poem anonymously himself. Two hundred and fifty copies were printed, bound in brown paper and sent to Bernard Quaritch, a London bookseller who specialized in Oriental literature. On April 9, 1859 a small notice appeared in *The Athenaeum* and *The Saturday Review* announcing the translation and that the price was one shilling. (A copy of this edition brought $9,000 in 1936.) FitzGerald sent out only three copies himself, to Cowell, Donne, and Browne. No replies from Donne or Browne have survived. FitzGerald told Charles Eliot Norton much later: "Cowell was naturally alarmed at it, he being a very religious man." No reviews appeared.

Two years later, Quaritch moved his bookshop and most of the unsold copies seem to have been lost in the process. A few that survived were dumped into the penny bargain box outside the shop. Someone bought a copy and showed it to Rossetti, and he and Swinburne bought copies and circulated them among their Pre-Raphaelite friends. Burne-Jones was delighted with it and showed it to Ruskin in 1863, who was so moved that he wrote a note to the anonymous translator and left it with Burne-Jones to deliver to the author when he was discovered. (Did no one think of asking Quaritch, one wonders, or had FitzGerald refused to have his name revealed?) A new edition was published in 1867, and that had better luck. Charles Eliot Norton visited Burne-Jones the following year and was told of the note Ruskin had written five years before. He took a copy of the new edition back with him to America, and wrote enthusiastically about it in *The North American Review*. As a result it had a brisk sale, but it was not until 1870 that an English magazine reviewed it. Ironically it was *Fraser's Magazine*, which had originally refused to publish extracts. The review was very laudatory, but the author still unidentified, and it was not until 1873 that the conversation between Norton and Carlyle occurred, which has already been described. Norton retrieved Ruskin's note from Burne-Jones and sent it to Carlyle who forwarded it to FitzGerald. It ran:

> I do not know in the least who you are, but I do with all my soul pray you to find and translate some more of Omar Khayyam for us. I never did—till this day—read anything so glorious to my mind as this poem. . . . More—more—please more.

FitzGerald wrote a note of thanks to Ruskin and commented to Norton: "It is really a funny little episode in the ten years dream." Though FitzGerald was publicly credited with the authorship in 1875, no edition published during his lifetime carried his name, and it was not until twenty years after his death, when Victorian orthodoxy had weakened, that the poem had its enormous popularity. At that time it fired one reader of future fame: "My first experience of intense excitement from poetry" wrote T. S. Eliot, "came when I was fourteen, not from anything put in my way by my work at school, but by happening to pick up at home a copy of FitzGerald's *Omar Khayyám.*"

The recognition of his achievement made no difference at all in FitzGerald's life. He met none of his admirers, though he corresponded regularly with Norton until his death, and sent him copies of his translations of Aeschylus and Sophocles and his edition of the poems of Crabbe. All these were also published anonymously, for his modesty was almost neurotic. When Fanny Kemble, in an article in *The Atlantic Monthly* praised him warmly as scholar and writer, and deprecated his diffidence, he insisted that the passage should be deleted when the essay was reprinted. When the Master of Trinity College asked him to send copies of all his publications for the College library, he did so, but with apologies: "I am a little ashamed of having made my leisure and idleness the means of putting myself forward in print." To Cowell he wonders why he *does* print these things, since nobody buys them and "I scarce now see the few I give them to." He concludes rather pathetically:

> But when one has done one's best, and is sure that that best is better than so many will take pains to do . . . one likes to make an end of the matter by Print.

After the fiasco of the marriage, FitzGerald took up his old drifting bachelor ways. His chief pleasure was sailing and he spent his summers at Lowestoft. His sailing, however, was not an active occupation, but merely another background for reading books. Giving the news that he has bought a boat, he adds:

> You must think I have become very nautical . . . haul away at ropes, swear, dance hornpipes etc: But it is not so: I simply sit in boat or vessel as in a moving chair, dispensing a little grog and shag to those who do the work.

No wonder he refers to his "obese ill-jointed carcase," but nevertheless he finds Lowestoft "a capital place for me; where one lies in the harbour, with all the sailors and fishers about one, and at night a glass of punch and a pipe at the 'Suffolk Inn'." And there's always "that old sea—talking to one, telling its ancient story."

For several years one of the great attractions of Lowestoft was the companionship of Joseph Fletcher, or "Posh," as he was called, a young fisherman, with a wife and children, with whom FitzGerald became completely infatuated. "While I am with him I feel young again" he says, and he writes enthusiastic descriptions of him to all his friends. He is "Nature's grandest type . . . a moving statue of strength and pliancy; like one of the Elgin marbles . . . and this man has a large simple soul and dignity of manner all of a piece." He insisted on having Posh's picture painted, to hang with those of Thackeray and Tennyson, "all three having a stamp of grandeur about them in their several ways and occupying great places in my soul." In 1867 FitzGerald financed the building of a herring-lugger for Posh, in which they were to be partners. "I daresay I had better have left all this alone," said FitzGerald, all too truly. For no one could have lived up to the qualities with which he had endowed Posh in his imagination, and the real Posh fell very far below them. He was a careless accountant and a heavy drinker, but FitzGerald will always find excuses for him:

> It makes me feel ashamed to play the judge on one who stands immeasurably above me in the scale, whose faults are better than so many virtues.

After three years the partnership was dissolved, as it was clear that Posh was not going to consult FitzGerald about its management. But that too becomes worthy: "The man is born to be master, not man, in any relation of life," and "he must rule alone, as is right he should too." FitzGerald continued to finance his protégé, losing money heavily, but again, he has "a different morality from ours . . . the man is royal, though with the faults of ancient Vikings." Posh evidently regarded his "gov'ner" as a queer old gold mine, who was always lecturing him on drink and mismanagement, but who would always forgive his lapses and supply the cash to meet his debts. Naturally he was totally uncomprehending of FitzGerald's need to love and be loved. In 1874 the "gov'ner" at last withdrew his financial support, but in 1877 he was still writing that "This is altogether the greatest man I have known." Two years later, however, he was forced to own that Posh seemed to be "sinking into disorder." One of FitzGerald's biographers reports that he ended in the workhouse, blaming his ill-fortune on FitzGerald, who had "spoilt" him.

As FitzGerald grew older it was only too clear that the life of withdrawal and of indolent ease he had chosen for himself failed more and more to bring him the satisfactions he had hoped for. In 1875 he quotes from the poet Crabbe:

> Man is but Man, and what he most desires
> Pleases at first: then pleases not, then tires!

Unlike Horace Walpole, FitzGerald had no Berry sisters to come and flatter and cheer his old age. Nor had he taken Dr. Johnson's advice to keep his friendships in constant repair. He remained devoted to Donne and Spedding but could not get up the energy to visit them in London. He corresponded regularly with Frederick Tennyson, who lived abroad, but after a meeting with him in early middle-life he writes:

> Really, if these little excursions . . . leave such a pleasant taste behind in memory, one should court them oftener. And yet perhaps the relish would be less . . .

"I get shyer and shyer even of those I knew," and when the Cowells returned from India in 1867, to live in Cambridge, where Cowell had been appointed Professor of Sanskrit, he is terrified at the idea of a reunion.

> I now see so few people, and those of the common sort, with whom I never talk of our old subjects; so I get in some measure unfitted for such converse, and am almost saddened with the remembrance of an old contrast when it comes.

He shies away from the idea of people visiting him as much as from the idea of visiting them. His immediate response to such suggestions is always an excuse: his house is not comfortable enough, or his nieces are staying with him, or he is ignorant of the latest books, plays, pictures: "I have all to ask and nothing to tell; and one doesn't like to make a pump of a friend." In 1879 his eldest brother died at Boulge Hall, three miles away, and he comments to Frederick Tennyson: "We were very good friends, of very different ways of thinking. I had not been inside his lawn gates these dozen years." Nor did he have any intercourse with the rest of the family except his sister, Mrs. Kerrich, whose death in 1863 was a great blow to him. He sold his yacht *Scandal*—so called, he said, because it was the staple product of Woodbridge—and "content myself with sailing on the river Deben, looking at the crops as they grow green, yellow, russet, and are finally carried away in red and blue waggons with the sorrel horses." And then October comes and "consigns me once more to cold, indoor solitude, melancholy and ill-health." He sends for a Persian dictionary from London, for "when winter comes I must take to some dull study to keep from suicide, I suppose." Winter in Woodbridge is "certainly next door to death," but when he thinks of joining Frederick Tennyson in Rome, the vision of packing, boats, railways, hotels, with the probable chance of disappointment, tips the scale: "Leave well—even 'pretty well'—alone: that is what I learn as I get old."

After living for sixteen years in his leaky cottage at Boulge, he spent another thirteen in cramped lodgings over a shop in Woodbridge. He could have moved to a comfortable farmhouse, which was offered him "in apple-pie order, with its good servants, garden etc"; but as he tells George Crabbe "I am afraid to leave the poor town with its little bustle. As one grows older, lonelier and sadder, is not a little town best?" Five years later, in 1867, he did buy and enlarge a house on the outskirts of the town, "which, after being built at near double the proper cost, is just what I do not want." He preferred to stay on in his lodgings, lending the house to his Kerrich nieces in the summer and being utterly careless of what happened to it when it was empty. All his pictures were injured by the damp, and in writing to his artist friend Samuel Lawrence he explains why: "I had no stove in the house and left doors and windows open long after they should have been shut." In 1873, however, his widower landlord took a second wife who refused to put up with FitzGerald as a lodger and he was forced to move. He chose to live in one room, "which I really prefer, as it reminds me of the cabin of my dear little ship"; and even when his nieces are in the rest of the house, his solitary life goes on: "They live by themselves, and I only see them now and then in the garden—sometimes not five minutes in the day." (Yet one of these must have been that "most delightful little girl in the world, chattering incessantly" who had delighted him so much twenty-five years before.) His eyesight deteriorated and he could not read at night, so he played solitaire for an hour or two in the evenings and hired a boy to come and read to him: "He stumbles at every third word and gets dreadfully tired, and so do I; but I renovate him with cake and sweet wine."

When FitzGerald was only fifty-seven, in commenting on the imminent death of a sister-in-law, he wrote: "If one only could escape easily and at once! For I think the fun is over: but that should not be." Old age came upon him very early. A photograph taken when he was sixty-four shows a heavy-jowled old man with a bald dome, a fringe of long, unkempt hair, fuzzy-looking side whiskers, a slipshod collar and cravat, and a melancholy droop to the finely cut mouth. He declared that it flattered him! In fact, he did not care what he looked like. He would walk about the town and its surroundings in an old Inverness cape, blue spectacles, and a top hat tied on with a handkerchief. Woodbridge regarded him as a harmless old lunatic. His old friends died: Donne, Spedding, Carlyle. It was in April 1883 that he went to London and saw the deserted house in Cheyne Row. In the middle of June he went for his annual visit to the Vicarage of George Crabbe. He went to bed early, and when he did not appear at breakfast, Crabbe went to his room and found he had died in his sleep.

But during all these years when he saw so few people, he wrote letters continually. He preferred that way of conversing with his friends. He worked at his translations; he made commonplace books of newspaper clippings, letters, poems, drawings, anecdotes, quotations. He read omnivorously, but he knew very well that he had none of the real creative zest for writing. When Bernard Barton had urged him to write, when he was in his early thirties, he had replied:

> I have not the strong inward call, nor cruel-sweet pangs of parturition, that prove the birth of anything bigger than a mouse . . . I am a man of taste, of whom there are hundreds born every year.

But if he left only one memorable work of art, he had the gift of creating himself fully in his letters as the man of the "very fine and delicate taste" noted by Tennyson. Like Lamb, he filled his letters with literary allusions and quotations and anecdotes, with discoveries of neglected writers, with talk of pictures and music, of actors and singers. His interest in the stage and opera and painting and concerts declined with the years as he became more and more of a recluse, but his appetite for books was never satiated. He would read his favorites over and over again, but his curiosity for new discoveries remained quite undimmed, though it lived in the past. And in spite of his own indolence, it is vitality and energy in writing that he loves. He recognized the melancholy hedonism of Omar Khayyám as universal: "It is a desperate sort of thing, unfortunately at the bottom of all thinking men's minds," yet in 1863, when he is working on the translation of another Persian poem, he exclaims to Cowell: "Oh dear, when I look into Homer, Dante, Virgil, Aeschylus, Shakespeare etc., those orientals look—silly! . . . These are the men!" He read and reread *Don Quixote,* Scott is among his favorite novelists, and he delighted in Dickens: "He always lights one up somehow." He finds his society in books: "All the people seem humming about me," and he identifies himself so closely with the characters in Trollope that he finds himself interrupting the story to exclaim: "No, no, she must have known she was lying!" or "He couldn't have been such a fool! etc." His prejudices, however, are as strong as his preferences. He could not understand the vogue for Jane Austen: "She is capital as far as she goes, but she never goes out of the parlour"; he made several unsuccessful attempts to get through *Middlemarch,* and found Hawthorne "painfully microscopic and elaborate on dismal subjects."

In contemporary poetry naturally he put Tennyson first, though he never forgave him for not living up to his early promise. He dismisses "the rank vegetation of Browning, Swinburne and Co.," and it is ironic that though it was the Pre-

Raphaelites who "discovered" his translation of Omar, FitzGerald had no interest at all in the movement and its offshoots. It is fortunate Ruskin did not know of his comment after a visit to the National Gallery in 1862: "the devotion of one whole room to Turner seems to me to be a national absurdity." Among the Romantics, he lost his early taste for Wordsworth and found him pompous and priggish; Shelley was "too unsubstantial for me; and poor Keats' little finger worth all his body: not to mention Byron, with all his faults." Like Lamb he responded warmly to the almost unknown Blake:

> I have lately bought a little pamphlet which is very difficult to be got, called *The Songs of Innocence,* written and adorned with drawings by W. Blake . . . who was quite mad, but of a madness that was really elements of great genius ill-assorted.

Naturally he loves the letter-writers. Mme. de Sévigné as "queen" of them, "once one has got over her perpetual harping on her daughter!" He does not mention Lady Mary, but had a deep admiration for Horace Walpole and in 1851 went to look at Strawberry Hill, finding it empty, with the rain coming through the roof and "gradually disengaging the confectionary battlements and cornices." Wesley's Journals are "one of the most interesting books in the language," and he comments on reading Wesley, Johnson, and Boswell consecutively: "three very different men whose lives extend over the same times and whose diverse ways of looking at the world they lived in make a curious study." He might have added Cowper, but comments only on Southey's biography of him as "a fearful book," and agrees with Southey in blaming Newton for Cowper's collapse, though regarding Newton himself as "a man of great power." He much prefers the letters to the essays of "dear Charles Lamb" and agrees with Thackeray in calling him "Saint Charles." He writes to Frederick Tennyson: "Beg, borrow or steal or buy Keats' Letters and Poems . . . most wonderful

. . . I only wonder they do not make a noise in the world . . . the strong, masculine sense and humour of the man!" To Norton and to James Lowell—whose two volumes of *Among my Books* were great favorites of his—he is constantly suggesting neglected writers or writings: Dryden's Prefaces; the poetry of Vaughan; *Clarissa,* which he would like to edit with "scissors and paste" and publish in a shortened form; "I want you to look at de Quincey," "certainly a remarkable figure and not yet decisively drawn," or "Give a look if you can at a memoir of Alfred de Musset written by his brother."

Though totally uninterested in the course of world affairs, sometimes he has startling intuitive perceptions. Commenting to Cowell on the fine things in Homer, he adds:

> Yet as I often think, it is not the poetical imagination, but bare Science that every day more and more unrolls a greater Epic than the Iliad: the history of the World, the infinitudes of Space and Time! I never take up a book of Geology or Astronomy but this strikes me.

And he shared with Walpole and Cowper a dislike of British colonialism:

> I say still, as I used, we have too much property etc. on our hands . . . we should give up something before it is forced from us. The world, I think, may justly resent our being and interfering all over the globe.

But it is the complete human being and not only the man of fine taste and insight who comes alive in the letters. A man always so sensitive to the beauties of his fenland country: the song of a bird, the light on the fields, the patterns of cloud, the ivy on an old wall. Even in the mess of his living room, delighting in color and form:

> On my table is a long-necked bottle, with three flowers just now in it . . . a tuft of rhododendrum, a tuft of scarlet geranium and a tuft of white gilliflower. Do you see these in your mind's eye?

Or he wants to find an old-fashioned rooster for his hens:

> Such as are seen in old story-books, and on churchvanes; with a plume of tail, a lofty crest and walk, and a shrill trumpet note of challenge; any splendid colours; black and red; black and gold; white and red and gold. Only so as to be "gay."

He does not have Lamb's talent for playing the fool at length, but a quiet humor about his restricted existence is always coming to the surface. He tells a few anecdotes of the broad, earthy humor of the country people—and one suspects more may have been suppressed by his early editors—but his own jokes are generally on himself. He interrupts a letter to Fanny Kemble from Lowestoft to watch a circus procession pass, and begins again: "This intoxication over . . . "; or reports:

> I see by a handbill in the grocer's shop that a Man is going to lecture on the Gorilla in a few weeks. So there is something to look forward to.

One evening he has to interrupt a reading of Hawthorne's Italian Notebooks because his boy-reader, though his father is a butcher, is terrified of a mouse in the room: "he is bringing some poisoned wheat for the mouse tomorrow." Or he describes a terrible *faux pas* on a rare visit to London, when unexpectedly he meets Anne Thackeray coming out of the Royal Academy,

> who took my hands as if really glad to see her father's old friend . . . I was taken aback somehow; and out of sheer awkwardness, began to tell her that I didn't care for her new novel!

He calls himself the great Blunderer, in matters like buying things he does not want, or failing to meet people he might have enjoyed; the blunders indeed are "so many luckily, that one has ceased to care for any *one*." But in spite of his reserve and detachment, a remark here and there reveals that, as he aged, he recognized his choice of his way of life as the biggest blunder of all. To Mrs. Allen, evoking the happy day of their youth, he confesses: "I might have profited more of those good days than I did; but it is not my talent to take the tide as it flows; and so all goes to worse than waste." Or to Mrs. Browne, widow of the friend who had been his ideal of full living:

> I can vouch with all the rest whom I have known like myself, that there is no happiness but in some settled plan of *action* before one.

He remained an amateur, a dilettante, with a Chekovian melancholy and a Chekovian inability to act, or to believe with passion in anything at all. When his sternly repressed emotions did explode into the ridiculous passion for Posh, he acted, but again in so blunderingly generous a way that he "spoilt" him for the simple life of a poor fisherman that was natural to him. He hungered for love in the midst of his self-chosen rejection of his fellows, and we can guess too that he really hungered for his just deserts of fame, as he saw the many less gifted and fastidious than himself attaining fulfillment as writers, scholars, or practical men of affairs. His deprivations only drove him further into retreat and forced resignation, as he lived, loyal and lonely, missing so many of the common pleasures of companionships, and without either a mystical faith or a creative drive strong enough to compensate for his self-destructive lack of vitality and purpose.

# Epilogue

AS A FINAL ironic comment on his life, FitzGerald chose for inscription on his gravestone: "It is He that hath made us and not we ourselves." It sounds a wry repudiation of responsibility, but perhaps he meant no more than that he was the victim of a temperament; that each human being is born with some inescapable individual pattern of consciousness and character which inevitably determines his response to future circumstance and environment. All of our letter-writers have revealed this truth. We have watched each striving to come to terms with a specific emotional inheritance and a specific set of circumstances which developed around him or her. Each set up defenses, which vary with each personality. Dorothy Osborne achieved a quiet resignation to a higher Will, that subdued her temperamental depression and her grief for the loss of her children. Cowper, convinced of a God who had decided to torture him in life and to consign him to eternal damnation hereafter, could do nothing but divert his faculties with activities which should temporarily obliterate his obsession. Swift was a Christian clergyman; he wrote prayers for use in Stella's sickness, but it is difficult to believe that his faith sustained him in his tormenting conflicts and frustrated ambitions, and finally he went mad. The others lived their lives without religious beliefs: Lady Mary, accepting her mistakes, continuing to make them, and dying garrulous but with an undefeated spirit;

Horace Walpole, who protected himself so carefully from emotions or from expressing those he had, but who nevertheless felt insecure and who nurtured resentments as keenly as anyone else; Lamb, choosing his path of human devotion in the clear knowledge of what it would mean, yet finally driven to escape his tragic loneliness in gin; Byron, helpless against his divided nature, which caused him to misspend his talents, ruin his marriage, and whose final assertion of creative activity was to end so quickly in disillusion and death; Jane Carlyle, fighting so gallantly against outer obstacles, but hindered so much by ignorance of the inner stresses that caused so many of them. FitzGerald, belatedly recognizing that his surrender to the temperamental urge towards withdrawal had impoverished his life beyond repair. Each reveals a living, unique individual in a particular setting; each found many satisfactions on the way and entertained himself and us with a wide variety of enjoyment and compensation. Yet did any die in the belief that he had fulfilled his potentialities, or managed to impose his own will on his experience?

Perhaps the deepest impression left on us from the reading of intimate letters, as we look back on these lives from the standpoint of posterity, is that the human condition does not change very much—if at all. And it is perhaps that, most of all, which creates within us so warm a fellow-feeling for these men and women of the past.

# Suggested Reading

*The Letters from Dorothy Osborne to Sir William Temple.* Everyman's Library. New York. E. P. Dutton & Co.

Cecil, David. *Two Quiet Lives.* New York. Bobbs-Merrill, 1947

Longe, Julia G. *Martha, Lady Giffard.* London. George Allen and Sons, 1911

Woodbridge, Homer E. *Sir William Temple.* Modern Language Association of America, 1940

---

*Journal to Stella.* Everyman's Library.

Davis, Herbert J. *Stella: a gentlewoman of the eighteenth century.* New York. Macmillan, 1942

Ehrenpreis, Irvin. *The Personality of Jonathan Swift.* Harvard University Press, 1958

Johnston, Denis *In Search of Swift.* Dublin. Hodges Figgis, 1959. [distributor in U.S., Barnes & Noble]

Le Brocuy, Sybil. *Cadenus.* A reassessment in the light of new evidence of the relationships between Swift, Stella and Vanessa. Dublin. Dolmen Press, 1903 [distributor in U.S., Oxford University Press]

---

*Letters of Lady Mary Wortley Montagu.* Everyman's Library.

Halsband, Robert. *The Life of Lady Mary Wortley Montagu.* Oxford. At the Clarendon Press, 1956

*Selected Letters of Horace Walpole.* Everyman's Library.
Lewis, Wilmarth Sheldon. *Horace Walpole.* Bollingen Series xxxv. Pantheon Books, 1960
———. *Collector's Progress.* New York. Alfred A. Knopf, 1951

---

*Selected Letters of William Cowper.* Everyman's Library.
Cecil, David. *The Stricken Deer.* London. Constable and Co., 1929
Quinlan, Maurice J. *William Cowper—a critical life.* University of Minnesota Press, 1953

---

*The Letters of Charles Lamb.* Everyman's Library. 2 volumes
Lucas, E. V. *The Life of Charles Lamb.* New York. Putnam's, 1905

---

Elwin, Malcolm. *Lord Byron's Wife.* New York. Harcourt Brace and World, 1962
Maurois, André. *Byron.* New York. Appleton & Co., 1930
Moore, Doris Langley. *The Late Lord Byron.* New York. J. B. Lippincott, 1961
Quennel, Peter. *Byron. A Self-Portrait: Letters and Diaries 1798–1824.* 2 volumes. New York. Scribner's, 1950

---

*Jane Welsh Carlyle:* a new selection of her letters—arranged by Trudy Bliss. London. Gollancz, 1949
Thomas Carlyle. *Letters to his Wife.* edited by Trudy Bliss. London. Gollancz, 1953
Hanson, Lawrence and Elizabeth. *Necessary Evil: the Life of Jane Welsh Carlyle.* New York. Macmillan, 1952

---

*Letters of Edward FitzGerald.* 4 volumes. edited by Aldis Wright. Macmillan, 1894–1901

*Letters of Edward FitzGerald to Fanny Kemble.* Macmillan, 1895

Blyth, James. *Edward FitzGerald and "Posh."* London. John Long, 1908

Terhune, Alfred McKinley. *The Life of Edward FitzGerald.* Yale University Press, 1947

# INDEX OF NAMES